S0-ARO-877

▲▲▲

Day and Overnight Hikes in the Great Smoky Mountains National Park

DAY AND OVERNIGHT
HIKES
IN THE
GREAT SMOKY
MOUNTAINS
NATIONAL PARK

▲▲▲

BY JOHNNY MOLLOY

MENASHA RIDGE PRESS
BIRMINGHAM, ALABAMA

Published by Menasha Ridge Press
Printed in the United States of America
First edition, third printing, 1998

Cover and text design by Carolina Graphics Group
Cover photograph by Frank Logue

Cataloging-in-Publication Data

Molloy, Johnny, 1961-
    Great day and overnight hikes in the Great Smoky Mountains
National Park / by Johnny Molloy.
        p.   cm.
    Includes bibliographical references and index.
    ISBN 0-89732-193-6
    1. Hiking—Great Smoky Mountains National Park (N.C. and
Tenn.)—Guidebooks. 2. Backpacking—Great Smoky Mountains
National Park (N.C. and Tenn.)—Guidebooks. 3. Trails—Great
Smoky Mountains National Park (N.C. and Tenn.)—Guidebooks.
4. Great Smoky Mountains National Park (N.C. and Tenn.)—
Guidebooks. I Title.
GV199.42.G73M64 1995
796.5'1'0976889—dc20   95-20513
                                                  CIP

▲ ▲ ▲
Menasha Ridge Press
P. O. Box 43059
Birmingham, Alabama 35243
(800) 247-9437
www.menasharidge.com

This book is for Lisa Ann Daniel,

who needs to take a hike.

▲▲▲

Acknowledgments

Most books have only one person's name below the title—the author's. But this book, as others, took a group effort to complete. First and foremost, I would like to thank Teresa Ann McSpurren for developing the idea while we were on a canoe trip in British Columbia. A Canadian, she had come to the Smokies often in her youth and loved them dearly. We met there and have remained friends ever since.

Thanks to Meredith Morris-Babb for steering me in the right direction, and to Mike Jones, Budd Zehmer and the rest of the folks at Menasha Ridge Press. I would be remiss not to thank W. W. Armstrong, Jennifer Dyer, Nancy McBee and my niece Jill Molloy for their help as well.

Table Of Contents

Introduction

The Great Smoky Mountains National Park: 270 miles of roads, 850 miles of trails, 500,000 acres of land. The numbers of flora and fauna are just as impressive: 50 species of mammals, 80 species of fish, 200 species of birds, 1,300 species of flowering plants, 2,000 species of fungi, and more. The park boasts seven trees of record dimensions among the upwards of 130 species that grow here. The diversity of ecosystems in this park is unmatched by any other temperate climates. Perhaps this is one of the primary reasons for its impressive designation as national park and international biosphere reserve.

To choose the Smokies as a place to spend your free time is a wise decision. And yet the Smokies can be intimidating, especially for the first-time visitor. Not only is there a lot of land to see, but with over nine million people annually, the Great Smoky Mountains National Park is the most visited national park in the American system. Quite intimidating indeed. Thus (the reason for) this book.

With so much land and so many people, discovering the beauty and solitude of this national park seems a hit-or-miss proposition. Where are the spectacular vistas? Where are the waterfalls and the old settlers' cabins? Where can I find solitude? Leaving it all to chance doesn't offer good odds for someone's all-too-brief vacation from the rat race. A lot of time spent daydreaming of this fleeting slice of freedom can turn into a three-hour driving marathon or a crowded and a noisy walk up the trail. With a little bit of planning and forethought and this book, you can make the most of your time in the Smokies.

This book presents over thirty day hikes for you to choose from. A few include the more popular areas, such as The Chimneys or Abrams Falls, but the majority of the hikes steer you toward infrequently visited areas, giving you the opportunity to enjoy your vacation on the trail instead of behind someone's car.

Two types of day hikes are offered: one-way and loop hikes. One-way hikes take you to a particular rewarding destination and back on the same trail. The return trip allows you to see everything from the opposite vantage point. You may notice the more minute features the second go-round, and returning at a different time of day can give the same trail a surprisingly different character.

To some, returning on the same trail isn't as enjoyable. Some hikers just can't stand the thought of covering the same ground twice with the hundreds of untrodden Smokies trail miles awaiting them. The loop hikes avoid this. Most of these hikes offer solitude to maximize your Smoky Mountain experience, though by necessity portions of some hikes traverse potentially popular areas. It should also be noted that loop hikes are generally longer and harder than the one-way hikes, but a bigger challenge can reap bigger rewards.

Day hiking is the best and most popular way to "break into" the Smokies backcountry, but for those with the inclination, this book offers ten overnight hikes. There are 102 designated backcountry sites and shelters available for those who want to capture the changing moods of the mountains. The length of these hikes, three days and two nights, was chosen to accommodate those who have only an extended weekend to travel. Certainly longer trips are viable. A backcountry permit is required for overnight stays in the backcountry. Certain campsites are reserved in advance. Permits are available at visitors centers or by calling (423) 436-1231.

When visiting the Smokies, it's a great temptation to remain in your car. While auto touring is a great way to get an overview of the park, it creates a barrier between you and the mountains. Windshield tourists, hoping for a glimpse of bears and other wildlife, often end up seeing the tail end of the car in front of them. And while roadside overlooks avail easy views, the drone of traffic and the lack of effort in reaching the views can make them less than inspirational. The Smokies were made for hiking.

The wilderness experience can unleash your mind and body, allowing you to relax and find peace and quiet. It also enables you to catch glimpses of beauty and splendor: a deer crashing through the underbrush as it clambers up a mountainside; the cabin remains of early settlers who scrabbled out a living among these woods; or a spectacular waterfall crashing above and below a trail. Out in these woods you can let your mind roam free, go where it pleases. This can't be achieved in a climate-controlled automobile.

The next few sections offer advice on how to use this book and how to have a safe and pleasant hike in the woods. The Smokies are a wild and beautiful place. I hope you will get out and enjoy what they have to offer.

—Johnny Molloy

How to Use This Guidebook

At the top of each hike is an information box that allows the hiker quick access to pertinent information: Quality of scenery, difficulty of hike, condition of trail, quality of solitude expected, appropriateness for children, as well as distance and approximate time of hike, and some of the highlights of the trip. The first five categories are rated using a five-star system. Below is an example of a box included with a hike:

Twentymile Loop

Scenery:	★★★★	Difficulty:	★★
Trail Conditions:	★★★	Solitude:	★★★★★
Children:	★★★★		

Distance: 7.4 miles round-trip
Hiking Time: 3:45 round-trip
Outstanding Features: waterfall, mountain streams,
deep woods

On this hike, four stars indicates that scenery will be picturesque, it will be a relatively easy climb (five stars for difficulty would be strenuous), the trail conditions are average (one star and the trail is likely to be muddy, narrow, or have some obstacle), you can expect to run into few if any people (with one star you'll likely be elbowing your way up the trail) and the hike is appropriate for able-bodied children (a one-star rating would denote that only the most gung ho and physically fit children should go).

The distance is absolute, but hiking time is an estimate for the average hiker. Loop hike times are given for the round-trip. One-way hike times are given for each way. Overnight hiking times include the burden of carrying a pack.

Following each box is a brief description of the hike. A more detailed account follows, where trail junctions, stream crossings and trailside features are noted along with their distance from the trailhead. This helps to keep you apprised of your whereabouts as well as to make sure you don't miss those features noted. You can use this guidebook to walk just a portion of a hike or combine the information to plan a hike of your own.

The hikes have been divided into one-way Day Hikes, loop Day Hikes and Overnight Hikes. The Day Hikes section has been further divided into Tennessee and North Carolina area hikes. Feel free to flip through the book, reading the descriptions and choosing a hike that appeals to you.

Weather

The Smoky Mountains offer four distinct seasons for the hiker's enjoyment, only sometimes it seems all four are going on at once, depending on where and at what elevation you are. Before your visit is over you will probably see a little bit of everything.

Be prepared for a wide range of temperatures and conditions, no matter the season. As a rule of thumb, the temperature decreases 3 degrees with every 1,000 feet of elevation gain. The Smokies are also the wettest place in the South. The higher elevations in the park can receive upwards of 90 inches of precipitation a year.

Spring, the most variable season, takes six weeks to reach the park's highest elevations. During this time, winter- and summer-like weather can be experienced, often in the same day. As the weather warms, thunderstorms become more frequent. Summer days typically start clear, and as the day heats up, clouds can build up, culminating in a heavy shower. Fall, the driest season, comes to the peaks in early September, working its way down, the reverse pattern of spring; warm days and cool nights are interspersed with less frequent wet periods.

Winter is the Smokies at their most challenging. Frontal systems sweep through the region, with alternately cloudy and sunny days, though cloudy days are most frequent in winter. No permanent snow pack exists in the high country, though areas over 5,000 feet receive five feet of snow or more per year. The high country can see bitterly cold temperature readings during this time. When venturing in the Smokies, it's a good idea to carry clothes for all weather extremes. See the safety section for more on clothing and equipment.

Clothing

There is a wide variety of materials to choose from. Basically, use common sense and be prepared for anything. If all you have are cotton clothes when a sudden rainstorm comes along, you'll get miserable quickly, especially in cooler weather. It's a good idea to carry along a light wool sweater or some type of synthetic apparel (polypropylene, Capilene, Thermax, etc.) as well as a hat. A poncho or other rain gear is appropriate too.

Footwear is another concern. Though tennis shoes may be appropriate in paved areas, the majority of the trails can be uneven and rough; tennis shoes may not offer enough support. Boots, waterproofed or not, are the footwear of choice. Sport sandals are becoming more popular, but these leave much of your foot exposed. A sliced foot far from the trailhead can make for a miserable limp back to the car.

Safety Concerns

To some potential mountain enthusiasts, the deep woods seem inordinately dark and perilous and full of hazards. It is the fear of the unknown that causes this anxiety. No doubt, potentially dangerous situations can occur in the outdoors as well as where you live, but as long as you use sound judgment and prepare yourself before you hit the trail, you'll be much safer in the woods than in most urban areas in our country. It is better to look at a backcountry hike as a fascinating discovery of the unknown, rather than a potential for disaster. Here are a few tips to make your trip safer and easier:

• Always bring food and water, whether you are day hiking or not. Food will give you energy, help keep you warm and may sustain you in an emergency situation until help arrives. And you never know if you will have a stream nearby when you are thirsty. If you drink water from a stream, treat it before drinking. The chance of getting sick from the organism known as giardia or other waterborne organisms is small, but there is no reason to take a chance. Boil or filter all water before drinking it.

- Stay on designated trails. Most hikers get lost when they leave the path. If you become disoriented, don't panic—this may result in a bad decision that will make your predicament worse. Retrace your steps if you can remember them, or stay put. Rangers check the trails first when searching for lost or overdue hikers.

- Bring a map, compass and lighter, and know how to use a map and compass. Should you become lost, these three items can help you stick around long enough to be found or get yourself out of a pickle. Trail maps are available at visitor centers and ranger stations. A compass can help you orient yourself, and a lighter can start a fire (for heat or for signaling).

- Be especially careful crossing streams. Whether you are fording or crossing on a footlog, make every step count. If using a footlog, hold onto the handrail, and be aware that footlogs are often moss covered and slippery. When fording a stream, use a stout limb as a third leg for balance. If a stream seems too high to ford, turn back.

- Be aware of the symptoms of hypothermia. Shivering and forgetfulness are the two most prevalent indicators of this cold weather killer. Hypothermia can occur even in the summer at higher elevations, especially when the hiker is wearing cotton clothing. If symptoms arise, get the victim shelter, warmth, hot liquids and dry clothes or a dry sleeping bag.

- Avoid bear-fear paralysis. The black bears of the Smokies are wild animals, hence unpredictable. If you see one, give it a wide berth; don't feed it and you'll be fine. There are no records of anyone being killed by a bear in the Smokies; most injuries have occurred when an ignorant visitor fed or otherwise harassed a wild bear.

- Always bring rain gear. The Smokies are the wettest place in the East, which is an important factor in the Smokies' remarkable biodiversity. Keep in mind that a rainy day is as much a part of nature as those idyllic ones you desire; and rainy days tend to cut down on the crowds. With the appropriate rain gear, a normally crowded trail can be a place of solitude. Do remember that getting wet opens the door to hypothermia.

- Take along your brain. A cool calculating mind is the single most important piece of equipment you'll ever need on the trail. Think before you act. Watch your step. Plan ahead. Avoiding accidents before they happen is the best recipe for a rewarding, stress-relieving hike.

- Ask questions. Park employees are there to help. It's a lot easier to gain advice beforehand rather than have a mishap away from civilization, when it's too late to amend an error. Use your head out there and treat the place as if it were your own backyard. After all, it is your national park.

Tips for Enjoying the Smokies

Before you go, call the national park for an information kit at (423) 436-1200. This will help get you oriented to the roads, features and attractions of the Smokies. These tips will make your visit enjoyable and more rewarding:

- Get out of your car and onto a trail. Auto touring allows a cursory overview of the park, and only from a visual perspective. On the trail you can use your ears and nose as well. This guidebook recommends some trails over others, but any trail is better than no trail.

- Use outlying trailheads to start a hike. First, you'll avoid the traffic of the main roads. Second, you'll most likely encounter more solitude on the outlying trails than on trails off the main roads. The Smokies are big, yet most visitors congregate in a few areas, so branch out.

- Investigate different areas of the park. The Smokies offer a wide variety of elevation, terrain and forest types. You'll be pleasantly surprised to see so many distinct landscapes in one national park. More detailed USGS maps are on sale at the visitors centers.

- Take your time along the trails. Pace yourself. The Smokies are filled with wonders both big and small. Don't rush past a unique salamander to get to that overlook. Stop and smell the wildflowers. Listen to the woods around you. Peer into the clear mountain stream. Don't miss the trees for the forest.

- We can't always schedule our free time when we want, but try to hike during the week and avoid the traditional holidays if possible. Trails that are packed in the summer are often clear during the colder seasons. If you are hiking on busy days, go early in the morning; it'll enhance your chances of seeing wildlife, too. The trails really clear out during rainy times. However, don't hike during a thunderstorm.

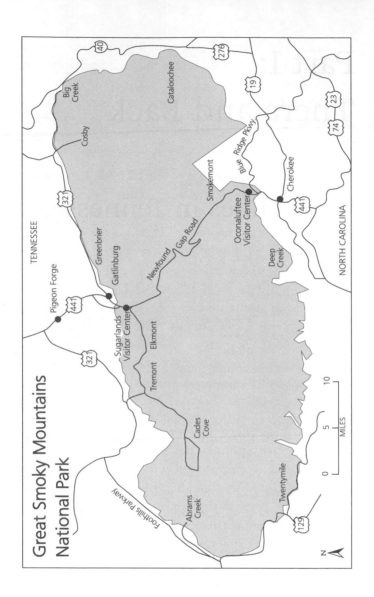

Part I:
There and Back

▲▲▲

Day Hikes in Tennessee

Abrams Falls from
Abrams Creek Ranger Station

Scenery:	★★★★★	Difficulty:	★★
Trail Conditions:	★★★	Solitude:	★★★
Children:	★★★		

Distance: 9.8 miles round-trip
Hiking Time: 5:30 round-trip
Outstanding Features: Abrams Creek gorge, Abrams Falls

It's hard to believe how few people you'll see going this way to such a popular destination as Abrams Falls. The sounds of Abrams Creek will keep you company for most of the hike, though. This hike starts on the Cooper Road Trail at the back of the Abrams Creek campground. Follow this jeep road through a hemlock forest across Kingfisher Creek, which can be a wet crossing in high water. At mile 0.9, turn right onto the Little Bottoms Trail, which is hardly more than a glorified pathway as opposed to the wide jeep road that is Cooper Road Trail.

Begin a short but steep climb. After topping a small ridge, begin descending. A short distance beyond the ridgetop on your right in a clearing between two of the many pine trees in the area is a spectacular view. On the trail's right, the gorge of Abrams lines up with the Smokies crest as a backdrop, allowing a view from the creek bottom to the mountaintop. Continue winding down until you come to the creek. Cross several small branches along Abrams Creek, reaching the Little Bottoms backcountry campsite, #17, at mile 2.5.

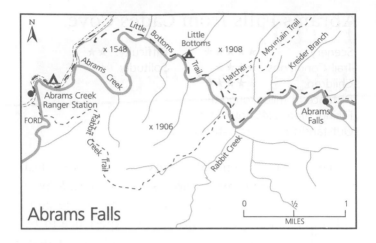

Abrams Falls

Watch your step on this spare trail as it once again climbs the steep side of the gorge filled with the rumblings of Abrams Creek below. Winding in and out of small side hollows, it intersects the Hatcher Mountain Trail at mile 3.1. Keep forward, descending briefly, to intersect the Abrams Falls Trail at mile 3.3.

To the right, the Hannah Mountain Trail begins with a difficult ford of Abrams Creek. Luckily, you continue forward along Abrams Creek, alternately crossing small creeks and looping rib ridges on a footpath wider than the Little Bottoms Trail, Abrams always within earshot. At mile 4.9, arrive at the Falls and the surprising crowds who have come 2.5 miles in the other direction from Cades Cove. Enjoy the falls and its immense plunge pool before returning to the Abrams Creek Ranger Station.

Directions: From Townsend, Tennessee, drive westward on US 321 and turn left onto the Foothills Parkway. Follow Foothills Parkway west to US 129, and turn left onto US 129 at Chilhowee Lake. Head south 0.5 miles to Happy Valley Road. Turn left on Happy Valley Road, following it 6 miles to Abrams Creek Road. Turn right on Abrams Creek Road and drive 1.0 mile to the campground, passing the ranger station. Cooper Road Trail starts at the rear of the campground. Park your car in the designated area near the ranger station.

Abrams Falls from Cades Cove

Scenery: ★★★★★   Difficulty: ★★
Trail Conditions: ★★★★   Solitude: ★
Children: ★★★★★
Distance: 5 miles round-trip
Hiking Time: 2:45 round-trip
Outstanding Feature: Abrams Falls

The hike to Abrams Falls from Cades Cove is an ideal beginner or family hike. Those seeking solitude may find the trail a bit peopled for their taste, but the sight and sounds of the wide falls are an experience to be shared by one and all. The trail to the falls, alternately coursing through rhododendron thickets and piny woods, parallels Abrams Creek most of the way, except when Abrams makes its quirky, nearly circular journey through the "horseshoe," a stretch of the creek famed for its fine trout fishing.

The trail leaves the Abrams Falls parking area and follows the crashing creek downstream. At mile 1.0, after traversing a few hills, the trail crosses a low point of Arbutus Ridge, which the creek has to go around, forming the horseshoe. Descend back down to Abrams Creek, alternately following close to the creek and farther up the ridgeside. This allows you to view the water-course from different perspectives as well as work your muscles a bit. Right before you reach the falls, cross

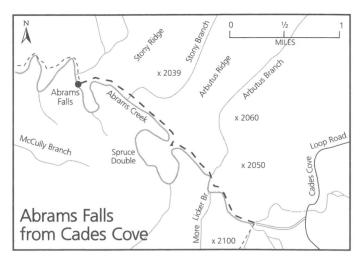

Wilson Branch on a flat-hewn footlog with a handrail.

At mile 2.5 take the short side trail to the falls. The wide plunge pool below the falls is nearly as impressive as the falls itself. In the summer this pool is a popular fishing and swimming hole. Abrams Falls, wide and powerful, descend in a roar of power and mist, quite a sight.

Directions: From the beginning of the Cades Cove Loop Road, drive 4.6 miles. Turn right onto a signed gravel road to the Abrams Falls parking area at 0.5 mile. The trail is in the right corner of the parking area.

Gregory Bald via Gregory Ridge

Scenery:	★★★★★	Difficulty:	★★★
Trail Conditions:	★★★★	Solitude:	★★★
Children:	★★★		

Distance: 10.8 miles round-trip
Hiking Time: 5:45 round-trip
Outstanding Features: Gregory Bald, views from grassy field, virgin forest

This hike is packed with features to satisfy even the most demanding hiker. On the way to Gregory Bald, world renowned for its wildflowers, pass along a mountain stream surrounded by old growth woodland, ascend a ridge, then pass historic Moore Spring, where an Appalachian Trail shelter once stood. It's a steady climb to the bald but well worth it.

Ascend quickly upon leaving Forge Creek Road, to join up with Forge Creek proper, crossing it on a footbridge. A little over a mile into the hike, an old growth forest of tulip trees and hemlocks begins to dominate the mountain scenery. Tulip trees, formerly known as tulip poplars or just poplars, have been renamed since they are not true poplars. Footlogs help you cross Forge Creek at mile 1.7 and 1.9. Just beyond the last crossing is the Forge Creek backcountry campsite, #12. Fill up with water here, as the rest of the way is dry until Moore Spring.

Leave the valley behind for the drier slope of Gre-

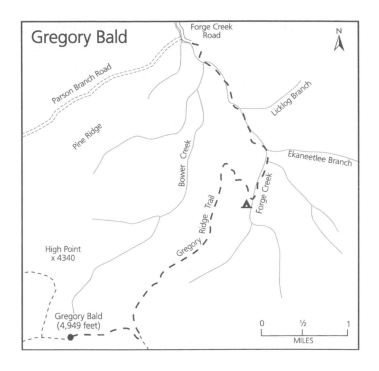

Gregory Bald

Forge Creek Road

N

Parson Branch Road

Pine Ridge

Bower Creek

Licklog Branch

Ekaneetlee Branch

Forge Creek

Gregory Ridge Trail

High Point
x 4340

Gregory Bald
(4,949 feet)

0   ½   1
MILES

gory Ridge. Top out on the ridge at mile 3.0. You've worked hard to get here, but the ridge keeps on rising. Winter views of the Smokies to your left keep your spirits up as you near Rich Gap and a trail junction, which is reached at mile 4.9.

To the right is the half-mile final ascent to Gregory Bald on the Gregory Bald Trail. To the left 0.1 mile, the Long Hungry Ridge Trail terminates from the Twentymile Ranger Station. Follow the unmarked path straight ahead, leading 0.3 mile to Moore Spring, where an Appalachian Trail shelter once stood before the A.T. was re-routed over Fontana Dam in the 1940s. The spring, in a small clearing that beckons a stop, is one of the Smokies' finest. Remember to treat all water before drinking.

Return to Rich Gap and the trail junction. Turn left up the Gregory Bald Trail, and soon you'll be on the bald at mile 5.4. Earlier in this century, cattle grazing here kept the forest from overtaking the bald, all the while maintaining a 15-acre open space. By the mid 1980s, the bald had shrunk to less than half that size. The park service decided to return the bald to its original size. Nowadays, don't be surprised if you see the park service actually mowing and cutting back growth at the bald's edges. However, many of the flame azalea bushes are left intact to bloom profusely during June. A hungry hiker can also sample the blueberries later in the summer. Except in inclement weather, Gregory Bald offers nearly 360-degree views year-round. Just a mile west is Parson Bald. To the south are the mountains of the Nantahala National Forest. Cades Cove lies below to the north, with east Tennessee and the Cumberland Mountains beyond.

Directions: Follow Cades Cove Loop Road for 5.5 miles, then turn right on Forge Creek Road. Follow it for 2.3 miles to the turnaround and the Gregory Ridge trailhead.

Rocky Top via Lead Cove

Scenery:	★★★★★	Difficulty:	★★★★
Trail Conditions:	★★★★	Solitude:	★★★★
Children:	★★		

Distance: 11.4 miles round-trip
Hiking Time: 6:00 round-trip
Outstanding Features: Spence Field, 360° view from
Rocky Top

This hike is the epitome of the old adage, "You reap what you sow." A lot of calories will be burned on the climb to your destination, but the view is as good as views get. Leave the lowlands via Lead Cove to intersect Bote Mountain Trail up to the Appalachian Trail, pass through Spence Field, and climb further still to the storied Rocky Top.

Leave Laurel Creek Road behind and step into history on the Lead Cove Trail, for what is a hike in the Smokies without a little history? Lead Cove derived its name from the ore that was extracted in the 1800s. Soon you pass an old homesite that lingers among the cool forest of the cove. Keep climbing somewhat steeply, leaving the bottom land behind to arrive at Sandy Gap and the Bote Mountain Trail at mile 1.8.

Turn right on the ridge-running jeep trail of Bote

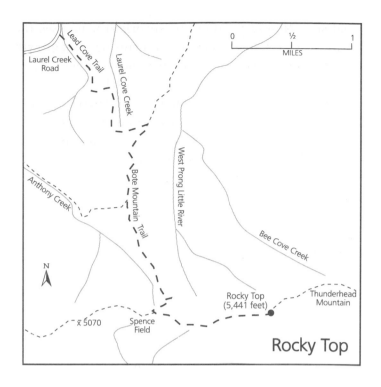

Rocky Top

Mountain. Ascend steadily through the fairly open pine-oak forest that allows intermittent views of Defeat Ridge to your left. At mile 3.0, you'll pass through the Anthony Creek Trail junction, then come to a jeep turn-around at mile 3.7. The trail becomes furrowed and narrow, passing through a seemingly continuous rhododendron tunnel to arrive at a saddle on Spence Field at mile 4.7.

Turn left on the famed Appalachian Trail, skirting Spence Field's eastern flank. Continue along the grassy meadow, passing the Jenkins Ridge Trail at mile 5.1. You'll descend briefly only to begin the final 0.6-mile climb to Rocky Top (elevation 5,441 feet) and its awesome views. Once on top, you'll understand why the view inspired the famed country song "Rocky Top," fight song for the University of Tennessee, a mere 30 miles away to the northwest. To your west, the meadows of Spence Field and the western crest of the Smokies, all the way to Shuckstack Mountain, stand out in bold relief. The views into Tennessee and North Carolina extend to the horizon. To your east the prominent peak by the imposing name of Thunderhead competes with the sky. Take in the view from this rock outcrop just as others have done for generations.

Directions: From Townsend, Tennessee, drive 5.6 miles from the Townsend "Y" right on Laurel Creek Road towards Cades Cove. The Lead Cove Trail is on your left just beyond a small parking area that extends on both sides of the road.

Buckhorn Gap via Meigs Creek

Scenery:	★★★★	Difficulty:	★★
Trail Conditions:	★★★	Solitude:	★★★★★
Children:	★★★		

Distance: 6.8 miles round-trip
Hiking Time: 3:00 round-trip
Outstanding Features: Meigs Creek valley

Once you leave the crowds at The Sinks behind, you'll probably have this intimate slice of the Smokies to yourself. This trail allows you to notice the smaller subtle features of a southern Appalachian mountain valley. Meigs Creek will surely catch your eye, as you cross it nearly 20 times. Not to worry, though, as most crossings are not difficult in times of normal water flow.

Once on the Meigs Creek Trail, swing past The Sinks, a popular swimming and sunbathing spot. Immediately drop into a boggy area, unusual for the Smokies, that was once part of the Little River. Begin ascending onto a dry piny ridge and notice the change in forest from the Little River valley. Wind back down and finally encounter the trail's namesake, Meigs Creek at mile 1.0.

The crossings begin here as the creek and trail merge amid a dark green forest interspersed with crashing cascades that flow beneath thickets of rhododendron. After the fourth crossing, a particularly comely falls announces its presence on your right. Continue fording, but stop to notice the clarity of the stream. The people who settled these coves revered their Smoky Mountain water and couldn't cotton to drinking "still" well water after they left their highland homes.

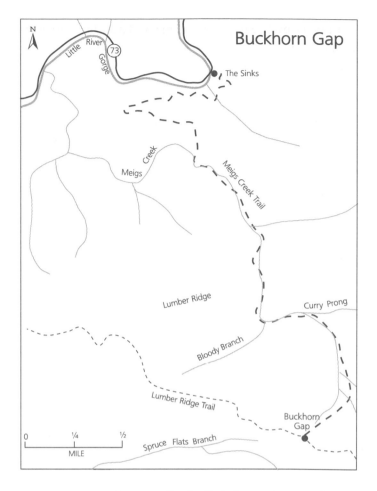

As you continue to climb slightly, Meigs Creek and the side creeks that feed it become smaller. Toward the head of the valley, you'll notice loggers left certain large hemlock trees behind. They were not considered commercially valuable in the early twentieth century and were left to become the giants of the forest they are today. The final climb at mile 3.3 signals your impending arrival to Buckhorn Gap at mile 3.4. You'll intersect the Meigs Mountain Trail, which goes to Elkmont, and the Lumber Ridge Trail, which goes to Tremont.

Directions: From the Sugarlands Visitor Center, drive 12 miles east on the Little River Road to The Sinks parking area on your left. The Meigs Creek Trail starts at the rear of the parking area.

Blanket Mountain via Jakes Creek

Scenery: ★★★★   Difficulty: ★★
Trail Conditions: ★★★★   Solitude: ★★★★
Children: ★★★
Distance: 8 miles round-trip
Hiking Time: 4:00 round-trip
Outstanding Features: limited views from Blanket
                              Mountain, ideal picnic spot

This hike starts along noisy Jakes Creek and ends atop Blanket Mountain, site of a former fire tower. Despite forest encroachment, an open glade still persists on top of the mountain and makes an ideal spot for a 4,600-foot-high country picnic on top of old Smoky. Follow a railroad grade most of your journey in this watershed of bygone logging and human settlement.

The park's last permanent lifetime resident, Lem Ownby, lived not far from the trailhead. He passed away in 1980, at the age of 91. When the park was formed, many residents deeded over their lands, then were given lifetime leases that allowed them to live out their lives in their cherished mountains.

The Jakes Creek Trail leaves the end of Jakes Creek Road, winding upward to meet the Cucumber Gap Trail at mile 0.3. Continue forward on the jeep road and pass through the Meigs Mountain Trail junction at mile 0.4. The trail begins rising a bit more steadily, crossing Waterdog Branch, then Newt Prong at mile 1.5. The trail narrows as you leave reforested cropland to switchback to the left, then again parallels high above Jakes Creek.

After crossing a couple of side branches, you come to the Jakes Creek backcountry campsite, #27, at mile 2.5. Continue working your way to the head of the watershed until you reach Jakes Gap and a trail intersection at mile 3.3. To your left the Miry Ridge Trail travels 4.9 miles to the Appalachian Trail. Turn right and trace the Blanket Mountain Trail.

As the trail winds its way up to the summit of Blanket Mountain, where a surveyor once hung a blanket as a marker to delineate Indian lands, you pass a rock outcrop on your left. Step atop the rocks and peer westward on nearby park land. Just beyond the outcrop, at mile 4.0, come to the summit of Blanket Mountain. The remains of the fire tower and cabin make a good table and backrest for the weary and hungry hiker. Blanket Mountain is an idyllic place to laze away a summer's day, escaping the heat of the lowlands.

Directions: From the Sugarlands Visitor Center, drive 4.9 miles on Little River Road to Elkmont. Turn left and follow the road 1.3 miles till you reach the Elkmont campground. Turn left at the sign for Little River and Jakes Creek trailheads. Drive 0.5 mile, then follow the right fork 0.5 mile farther to the end at the parking area. Jakes Creek Trail starts at the left rear of the parking area.

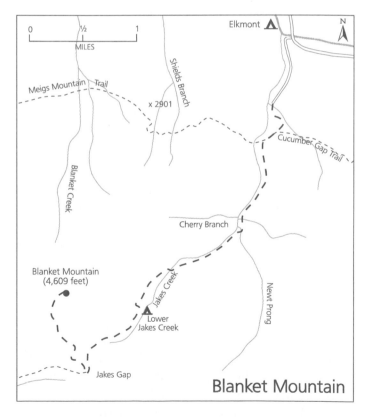

Laurel Falls

Scenery: ★★★★★   Difficulty: ★
Trail Conditions: ★★★★★   Solitude: ★
Children: ★★★★★
Distance: 2.6 miles round-trip
Hiking Time: 1:30 round-trip
Outstanding Features: Laurel Falls

This short, moderate hike is so popular that the park service has paved the trail to the falls. This makes the footwork easier but detracts from the wilderness aspect of the hike. However, this unusual waterfall is worth walking to; the trail bisects it, the falls cascading above and below the trail.

Leave Fightin' Creek Gap (elevation 2,300 feet) on the Laurel Falls Trail. Swing west around an unnamed ridge into the hollow of Pine Knot Branch at mile 0.4. Veer north at the point of the ridge, where each side of the trail provides contrasting topography. Below to your left flows Laurel Branch through a steep gorge cut by time and the elements. On the trail's right, an abrupt rock face stands testimony to the blasting work done by Depression era trail crews that enables you to reach the falls easily.

After the park's inception in the 1930s, the Civilian Conservation Corps was engaged to help develop the

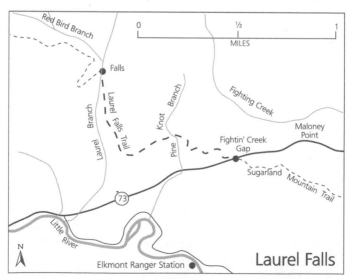

Smokies. This government-works unit, designed to give jobs to those unemployed during the Great Depression, built much of the park's infrastructure, including roads, government buildings and trails, as well as this section of the Laurel Falls Trail.

The trail climbs a total of 300 feet by the time you reach Laurel Falls at mile 1.3. Observe the falls above and below. To check out the falls in its entirety, rock hop across Laurel Branch amidst the spray and continue beyond the falls a hundred yards or so, then look back at the 75-foot drop. Just imagine the time it took for the water to wear down the Smokies to the form we see them today.

Directions: From the Sugarlands Visitor Center, drive 3.8 miles on Little River Road to Fightin' Creek Gap. The Laurel Falls Trail starts at the rear of the right hand parking area.

The Chimney Tops

Scenery:	★★★★★	Difficulty:	★★★
Trail Conditions:	★★	Solitude:	★
Children:	★★★		

Distance: 4 miles round-trip
Hiking Time: 2:15 round-trip
Outstanding Features: old growth trees, 360° view from the Chimney Tops

If you don't mind some company on the trail, this short but steep hike is nothing less than spectacular. Leaving the traffic behind on Newfound Gap Road, sharply ascend via a series of footbridges set amid some old trees, and emerge on top of the Smokies' single most recognizable rock formation: the twin spires of the Chimney Tops, which provide a dramatic view of the surrounding landscape.

This steep trail starts by going down. Leave the parking area on the Chimney Tops Trail and follow the path down to Walker Camp Prong, where a footbridge awaits your crossing. Continue on, entering Beech Flats Cove, to cross Road Prong on two footbridges in short

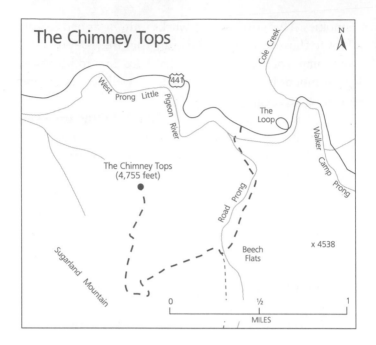

The Chimney Tops

Cole Creek

N

West Prong Little Pigeon River

441

The Loop

Walker Camp Prong

The Chimney Tops
(4,755 feet)

Road Prong

Sugarland Mountain

Beech
Flats

x 4538

0   ½   1

MILES

succession. Just after the hike's fourth footbridge, you'll come to the Road Prong Trail junction at mile 0.9.

Turn right, staying on the Chimney Tops Trail, which steepens considerably. Due to the heavy traffic, the trail is rutted and has toe-grabbing roots along the way, so watch your step. But don't forget to look up every now and then to admire the old growth trees that accompany you on your way up.

At mile 2.0, top out on the rib ridge of The Chimneys that extends from Sugarland Mountain to your left. To your right are the twin peaks that reminded some pioneer long ago of a chimney on a house. There is actually a hole in the rock big enough to fall in. The native Cherokee fancied the rock formation to be the branched horns of a deer, so they called this place Forked Antler. Be very careful as you climb around and up the right of this 4,755-foot-high rock formation.

To your east, beyond the second chimney, stands Mount LeConte. To your west is the wooded wall of Sugarland Mountain. Southward is Mount Mingus. Down below to the north is the valley of the West Prong of the Little Pigeon River and Newfound Gap Road, your return destination.

Directions: From the Sugarlands Visitor Center, drive 6.7 miles on Newfound Gap Road. The Chimney Tops parking area is on your right.

Alum Cave Bluff

Scenery:	★★★★★	Difficulty:	★★
Trail Conditions:	★★★★	Solitude:	★
Children:	★★★★		

Distance: 4.6 miles round-trip
Hiking Time: 2:30 round-trip
Outstanding Features: Arch Rock, Alum Cave Bluff

Nature's beauty and power are well represented on this hike. The unhurried growth of an ancient forest coupled with the nearly imperceptible effects of freezing and thawing is mingled with the instantaneous actions of two landslides that occurred in the latter half of this century, the latest slide occurring in 1993. The combination of these events result in such a feature-packed hike that you'll be glad to make a return journey just to take it all in again.

Begin at the Alum Cave Trail and immediately enter an old growth forest around Walker Camp Prong, which you soon cross on a footlog. Walk parallel to Alum Cave Creek for nearly a mile after crossing it on a footlog. Cross Alum Cave Creek on another footlog at mile 1.0.

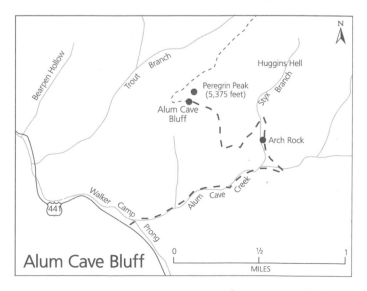

Alum Cave Bluff

The trail swerves left and begins to follow Styx Branch. To your left are the boulder and log remnants of the 1951 landslide that followed a rainstorm of major proportions, even by Smoky Mountain standards. Shortly after this you'll walk through the evidence of the more recent "gully washer." In the summer of 1993, a storm struck high on Mount LeConte. The resultant rain saturated the ground and roared down the Styx Branch valley, bringing with it a mass of LeConte, wiping out all that stood in its way.

Next, come to one of nature's more time-consuming projects, Arch Rock, at mile 1.5. A set of stone stairs aids your passage through one of the few natural arches inside the park. Continue ascending, and at mile 1.9, come to an area covered with small, low bushes known as a heath bald.

After leaving the bald, arrive at Alum Cave Bluff (elevation 5,000 feet), at mile 2.3. This feature was never a cave but rather an overhang that was mined for saltpeter during the Civil War. You can usually smell the sulfur in the air at the bluff. In winter, large icicles form at the top of the overhang, crashing down when the air warms. Nature is constantly at work on the Alum Cave Bluff Trail.

Directions: From the Sugarlands Visitor Center, drive 8.6 miles on Newfound Gap Road. The Alum Cave Bluff parking area is on your left.

Silers Bald

Scenery:	★★★★★	Difficulty:	★★★
Trail Conditions:	★★★★	Solitude:	★★★
Children:	★★		

Distance: 9.6 miles round-trip
Hiking Time: 5:00 round-trip
Outstanding Features: high country, views all along hike, Silers Bald

This hike fairly exudes the aura of the high country, as you traverse in and out of the spruce-fir forest that cloaks only the highest mantles of this land.

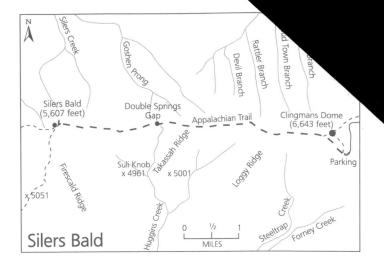

Silers Bald

Straddle the very spine of the state line ridge, which offers windswept vistas into both states that comprise the Smoky Mountains. Once you've reached the top of Silers Bald, you can look back and see where you started—Clingmans Dome parking area.

Start your hike at the Clingmans Dome parking area, leaving on the Forney Ridge Trail. At mile 0.1 veer right on the Clingmans Dome Bypass Trail. Climb moderately to mile 0.6, where you'll intersect the Appalachian Trail near Mount Buckley (elevation 6,500 feet). Continue west on the A.T., dropping through an old burned-over section with views. Drop into a saddle then briefly ascend again, topping out at a rock outcrop that makes a wonderful bench. Sit awhile and look far into North Carolina.

Enter the spruce-fir forest again, moving downward all the while. It is nearly always wet and cool here, pungent with the aroma of rich earth and growing and decaying vegetation. After a brief level section come to the Goshen Prong Trail junction at mile 2.7. Continue your descent on the A.T. to arrive at the Double Springs Gap Trail shelter at mile 3.1. A small clearing stands in front of the shelter. As you arrive at the shelter, the spring to your left, in North Carolina, is the easiest place to obtain water.

Leave the shelter behind and climb atop Jenkins Knob, jumbled with beech trees. Beech leaves turn

n the tree throughout the win-
...d. Below the knob you'll come to
...elch Ridge lines the horizon to your
...into North Carolina. Pass through The
...e the state line ridge becomes barely wide
... a footpath.

...Welch Ridge Trail junction intersects the A.T.
at mile 4.4. Begin the final push to arrive on top of Silers
Bald (elevation 5,607 feet) at mile 4.8. Look back at the
rugged crest of the Smokies. As you arrive at Silers Bald,
a small side trail to your right allows long views into
Tennessee. The A.T. continues down the shrinking bald
to your left, which the park service is allowing to become reforested. Relax in what remains of the field and
take it all in.

Directions: From Newfound Gap, drive 7 miles to the
end of Clingmans Dome Road. The Forney Ridge Trail
starts at the tip end of the Clingmans Dome parking
area.

Charlies Bunion

Scenery:	★★★★★	Difficulty:	★★
Trail Conditions:	★★★	Solitude:	★★
Children:	★★★		

Distance: 8.0 miles round-trip
Hiking Time: 4:00 round-trip
Outstanding Features: high country, views, Charlies
Bunion

Many people believe the view from Charlies Bunion is the park's finest. Unlike a view from a fire tower
or a rounded peak, Charlies Bunion boasts a vista from
a cliff face with an abrupt drop of more than 1,000 feet.
The hike to the Bunion offers views of its own, interspersed with high country forest.

Unusual for the older Appalachian Range, the pre-
cipitous Charlies Bunion is the result of two events in
the 1920s. A devastating fire raged over this area in 1925,
denuding the thin soil of the vegetation that held it in
place. In 1929 heavy rains resulted in a landslide of the

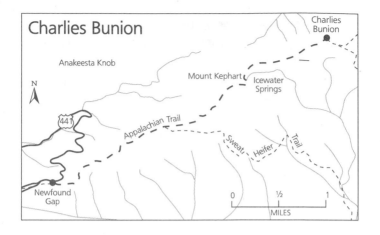

Charlies Bunion

burned-over area, exposing the rock face we see today.

Head east from Newfound Gap on possibly the most hiked quarter-mile of the entire Appalachian Trail. However, as you climb away from the gap, the throngs soon disappear. The trail is rocky and often wet, so use caution as you continue to wind up the side of Mount Kephart. The southern flank of Mount LeConte lies to your left.

At mile 1.7, you'll come to a level area and the Sweat Heifer Trail junction. Stay on the A.T., which is often muddy here as it passes the 6,000-foot elevation mark, then descends to the Boulevard Trail junction at mile 2.7. Continue on the Appalachian Trail as the evergreens crowd the path, opening up at the Icewater Springs trail shelter at mile 2.9. Nowadays the shelter is open only to "thru" hikers, those intending to cover the entire 2,100 miles of the A.T. Just beyond the shelter is Icewater Springs. Its name is well deserved.

Beyond the spring, a half-mile decline on a rocky wet slope leads to a narrow stretch of the main ridge veering left, arriving at a trail junction at mile 4.0, just before Charlies Bunion. To the right is the A.T. Carefully follow the narrow trail to your left 100 yards and arrive at Charlies Bunion.

Below you is the remote Greenbrier area of the park. To your left is Mount LeConte. A clear day will allow an unparalleled view into the hills of east Tennessee. At your feet, dark-eyed juncos and eastern chipmunks will vie for some of your trail mix. This is a great place to appreciate just how high the Smoky Mountains are.

Directions: From the Sugarlands Visitor Center, drive 13.1 miles to Newfound Gap. The trailhead is at the parking area's left, near the large stone podium with the plaque on it. From the Oconaluftee Visitor Center, drive 16 miles to Newfound Gap. The trailhead is at the far end of the parking area as you come from North Carolina.

Injun Creek from Greenbrier

Scenery:	★★★★	Difficulty:	★
Trail Conditions:	★★★★	Solitude:	★★★★★
Children:	★★★★		

Distance: 6.4 miles round-trip
Hiking Time: 3:30 round-trip
Outstanding Features: old homesites, small creeks,
old steam engine

Take a walk through time on this hike, which skirts the lower reaches of Mount LeConte, passing a collection of former farms and homesites that dot the Greenbrier area. The hike culminates at the Injun Creek backcountry campsite, above which lies an old steam engine, a relic of the settler days in the Smokies. This isolated, historic walk is one of the most underrated and underused in the park.

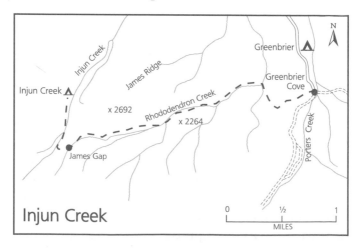

Your hike starts on the Grapeyard Ridge Trail, which follows an old road used by area settlers. You'll pass rock walls and more old roads that splinter off the trail. Ascend a small ridge, and at mile 0.6, you'll find an old homesite and the remains of a chimney. The trail follows a small rill leading to Rhododendron Creek. When you enter an old field, you will begin the first of several crossings of Rhododendron Creek and its tributaries, none of which are deep, though you may wet your boots a bit.

Wind up the creek valley, noting homesites on both sides of the trail. The 1931 topographic map of the Smokies shows eleven homesites in the Rhododendron Creek watershed. Rhododendron, the creek's namesake, constrict the path in areas near the creek, but the trail opens up away from water.

At mile 2.2, leave Rhododendron Creek and begin the ascent to James Gap. Another homesite sits in the saddle of James Gap at mile 2.8. Enter the Injun Creek watershed. As you descend, the inspiration for the name Injun Creek appears in a rivulet on your right. The body and wheels of a tractor-like steam engine lie upturned, water running beneath the engine's rusted hulk. Somewhere in the naming of this creek, an errant mapmaker thought the name Injun Creek referred to Indians rather than this old steam engine that made its final turn in the Smoky Mountains.

The former road-turned-trail descends to reach the side trail to the Injun Creek campsite, #32. Turn right on the side trail to the camp at mile 3.2, where there is yet another homesite. Walk around and look at the lasting changes the settlers made on the land, such as leveling the ground with rock walls. The campsite makes for a good break spot. On your return journey, try to visualize how this area will look once the forest reestablishes itself over this area of the Smokies.

Directions: From Gatlinburg, drive 6 miles east on US 321 to Greenbrier. Turn right at the Greenbrier sign and follow Greenbrier Road 3.1 miles to the intersection with Ramsey Prong Road, which crosses a bridge to your left. Park just before the intersection. The Grapeyard Ridge Trail starts on the right side of Greenbrier Road.

Brushy Mountain

Scenery: ★★★★★   Difficulty: ★★★
Trail Conditions: ★★★★   Solitude: ★★★★
Children: ★★
Distance: 11.4 miles round-trip
Hiking Time: 5:30 round-trip
Outstanding Features: old homesites, views from atop
                     Brushy Mountain

This hike passes through old farming areas, ascends through dry ridge country and a hemlock forest, and arrives at Trillium Gap. A short climb leads you to the top of Brushy Mountain, where views await amid a heath-bald plant community. The more than 2,500-foot climb is steady, but the varied forest types and the view at the end are well worth the effort.

Leave Greenbrier Road on the Porters Creek Trail. The crashing Porters Creek will be your companion as you gently rise, passing the Ownby Cemetery about a half-mile from the trailhead. The Brushy Mountain Trail junction is reached at mile 1.0. Follow Brushy Mountain Trail as it leaves the junction at the far end of a loop and enters an old farm community located in Porters Flat. Old rock walls, chimneys and discarded metal items are all that remain of lives led in the shadow of nearby Mount LcConte.

At mile 2.2, a small side trail leads down on your right to Fittified Spring, whose name is a first-rate example of mountain-folk vernacular (the spring has apparently steadied its flow nowadays). The trail passes near Long Branch but veers back south while leaving Porters Flat behind. The climb to Brushy Mountain remains steady as the trail enters a pine-oak forest, so prevalent on south-facing slopes.

At mile 3.1 a large boulder to your right offers a nice combination vista and rest spot. Continue climbing and cross Trillium Branch twice, where the forest

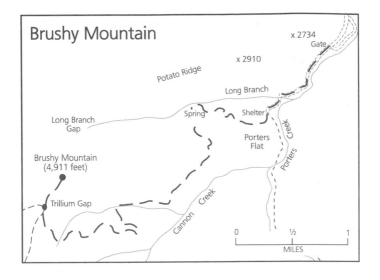

Brushy Mountain

x 2734
Gate

x 2910

Potato Ridge

Long Branch

Long Branch
Gap

Spring

Shelter

Porters
Flat

Porters Creek

Brushy Mountain
(4,911 feet)

Trillium Gap

Cannon Creek

0   ½   1

MILES

becomes dominated by hemlock trees. At mile 5.5, you'll reach grassy Trillium Gap. This is one of those mountain places with a perpetual cool breeze that demands a stop to absorb the ambiance beneath the beech trees.

To reach the top of Brushy Mountain, veer right from the gap and follow the path beneath the tunnel of rhododendron and mountain laurel, which are the primary components of the heath-bald community. Come to an opening in the bald at mile 5.7. Brushy Mountain offers panoramas both above and below your 4,900-foot elevation. Above and to your south is the imposing bulk of Mount LeConte. To your east lies Porters Creek valley where you started. Below, to the north, are Gatlinburg and east Tennessee.

Directions: From Gatlinburg, drive 6 miles on US 321. Turn right at the Greenbrier sign and drive 4 miles to the end of Greenbrier Road. The Porters Creek Trail starts at the back of the parking area.

Ramsay Cascade

Scenery:	★★★★★	Difficulty:	★★★
Trail Conditions:	★★★	Solitude:	★★
Children:	★★★		

Distance: 8.0 miles round-trip
Hiking Time: 4:00 round-trip
Outstanding Features: old growth, forest, falls at end
of trail

This is a popular hike with a well-deserved reward, not only at the end, but also during the hike itself. It starts out with a slight upgrade, then climbs more steeply as it nears the falls. The steeper portion of the trail is lined with old growth trees that never saw the logger's axe or any settlement, for that matter. The area remains as it has been for ages.

Start your hike on the south side of the Middle Prong of the Little Pigeon River on the Ramsay Cascade Trail. Cross over the prong on a very long footbridge, and wind your way past Ramsay Branch, which flows from Greenbrier Pinnacle, shading the trail to your left. At mile 1.5, the trail comes to a turnaround. The Greenbrier Pinnacle Trail, no longer maintained, splits off to the left. The Ramsay Cascade Trail continues forward and begins to climb more steeply.

Cross back to the south side of Ramsay Prong on a footlog at mile 3.1, then climb away from the main creek

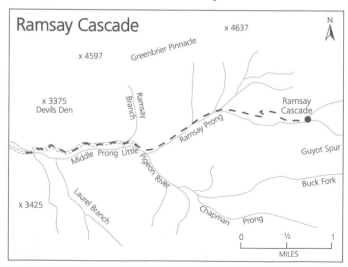

to cross and re-cross a small branch, continually gaining elevation. This is the valley of the big trees: tulip trees, Carolina silverbells, eastern hemlocks and others. Traverse Ramsay Prong yet again on another footlog as you near the cascades, at mile 3.7. Exposed roots on the hiker-worn path can make the trail tricky, especially while you're looking around at all the big trees.

Plunging down the green valley, between the high ridges of Guyot Spur and Pinnacle Lead, is Ramsay Cascade (elevation 4,300 feet), at mile 4.0. Though it falls less than 100 feet, the cascade sends out quite a spray. Picnickers and trail-weary hikers always seem to find a great view from a suitable rock to watch this natural water show.

Directions: From Gatlinburg, drive 6 miles east on US 321 to Greenbrier. Turn right at the Greenbrier sign and follow Greenbrier Road 3.1 miles to the intersection with Ramsay Prong Road, which crosses a bridge to your left. Turn left on Ramsay Prong Road and follow it for 1.5 miles to the parking area at the end of the road. The Ramsay Cascade Trail starts at the rear of the parking area.

Mount Cammerer via Low Gap

Scenery:	★★★★★	Difficulty:	★★★
Trail Conditions:	★★★	Solitude:	★★★★
Children:	★★		

Distance: 10.8 miles round-trip
Hiking Time: 5:15 round-trip
Outstanding Features: historic fire tower, views from
atop Mount Cammerer

Formerly called White Rock by Tennesseans and Sharp Top by Carolinians, this mountaintop rock outcrop was renamed by the park service after Arno B. Cammerer, former director of the National Park Service. No matter the name, this peak has incredible panoramas from its place on the Smokies crest. An historic wood and stone fire tower, long in disuse, is slated for restoration by a group known as Friends of the Smokies.

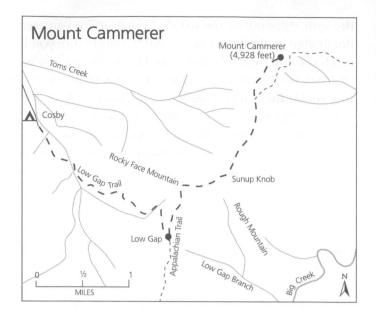

Mount Cammerer

This restoration will make Mount Cammerer an even more desirable destination.

The trek to Cammerer starts in Cosby at the hiker parking area on the Low Gap Trail. Follow the newer path, which skirts the campground for 0.3 mile to the old Low Gap Trail, once maintained as a road to the fire tower. Enter farmland-turned-woodland to cross Cosby Creek on a footbridge at mile 0.9.

The trail begins a steady but not too steep climb toward the Smokies crest. The wide roadbed allows you to look around without having to watch your every step. At mile 1.3, the trail makes the first of several switchbacks amid a nearly virgin forest. Cross Cosby Creek (now tiny) again at mile 2.5, as the trail works its way toward Low Gap where it meets the Appalachian Trail at mile 2.9.

At Low Gap, turn left on the A.T. and resume your ascent. This section of the A.T. is much less used than the section near Newfound Gap. After a mile of steady climbing, the A.T. levels out near Sunup Knob at mile 3.9. The trail is as level as trails come in the Smokies, rising slightly near the junction with the Mount Cammerer Trail at mile 4.9.

Turn left on the Mount Cammerer Trail and follow

the spur ridge out of the wooded junc
dominated by mountain laurel. After a
reach the outcrop and tower at mile 5.
to climb up the tower to enjoy the vi
ting rocks, for you can see in every
outcrop. The rock cut of I-40 is visible to your east.
Mount Sterling and its fire tower are to your south. In
the foreground to the north is the appropriately named
Stone Mountain. Beyond Stone Mountain, to the
horizon's end, lies Tennessee. Maybe a place this spectacular does deserve three names.

Directions: From Gatlinburg, take US 321 east until it
comes to a "T" intersection with Tennessee Highway
32. Turn right on Tennessee Highway 32 and follow it a
little over a mile, turning right into the signed Cosby
section of the park. At 2.1 miles, come to the hiker parking area to the left of the campground registration hut.
The Low Gap Trail starts in the upper corner of the
parking area.

▲▲▲

Day Hikes
in North Carolina

Andrews Bald

Scenery: ★★★★★   Difficulty: ★
Trail Conditions: ★★★★   Solitude: ★★
Children: ★★★★★
Distance: 3.6 miles round-trip
Hiking Time: 1:45 round-trip
Outstanding Features: spruce-fir forest, Andrews Bald

This is one of the Smokies' finest hikes. The trip
passes through an extraordinary spruce-fir forest to the
grassy field of Andrews Bald. Resplendent with stun-
ning views, this is an ideal backdrop for a picnic in the
sky. Andrews Bald is one of only two grassy fields in

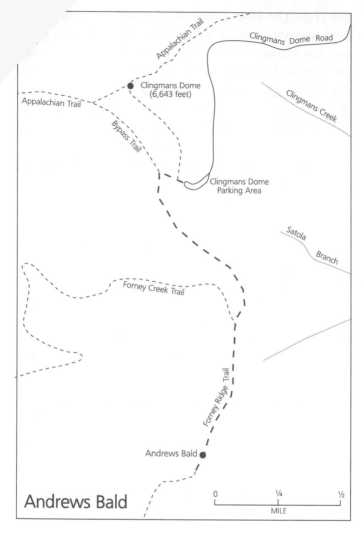

Andrews Bald

the Smokies that the park service maintains in their "original" state. The origin of these fields is not clear, although fire, Indians and cattle are thought to be possibilities.

After leaving the Clingmans Dome parking area on the Forney Ridge Trail, you zig zag through an evergreen forest reminiscent of Maine or Canada. Make sure you veer left away from the Clingmans Dome Bypass Trail 0.1 mile into the hike. The Forney Ridge Trail descends along a rocky section that allows views southward, and at mile 1.0, intersects the Forney Creek Trail.

Continue forward along the undulating and rocky ridge to arrive at the southern end of Andrews Bald at mile 1.8. The lush grassy field (elevation 5,800 feet) beckons you to lie down, but then that would deny you the expansive views of the southern range of the Smokies and beyond, as far south as the clarity of the sky allows. This bald, the Smokies' highest, also offers marvelous flower displays in June, as well as blueberries and blackberries in late summer.

Directions: From Newfound Gap, drive 7 miles to the end of Clingmans Dome Road. The Forney Ridge Trail starts at the tip end of the Clingmans Dome parking area.

Mount Sterling
via Mount Sterling Gap

Scenery:	★★★★★	Difficulty:	★★
Trail Conditions:	★★★★★	Solitude:	★★★★
Children:	★★★		

Distance: 5.6 miles round-trip
Hiking Time: 2:45 round-trip
Outstanding Features: excellent views from Mount Sterling tower

At 5,842 feet, the top of Mount Sterling is adorned with one of only two original fire towers that hikers can climb to capture panoramas above the treetops. And the views from the spruce-fir high country of Sterling are limited only by the clarity of the sky. The hike begins at Mount Sterling Gap and follows a short but sloping old jeep road to Mount Sterling Ridge and the high country. From the ridge top, a short climb takes you to the top and the tower.

Leave Mount Sterling Gap (elevation 3,890 feet) and begin climbing steeply up the wooded mountainside. The trail levels out a bit as it comes to an open area and the Long Bunk Trail junction at mile 0.4. Resume climbing and make a sharp switchback to the right at mile 0.7.

The climb doesn't slacken much as it switchbacks further up the mountain until it reaches the Mount Sterling Ridge Trail junction in a small grassy area at mile

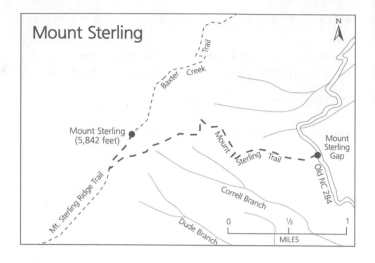

Mount Sterling

Baxter Creek Trail

Mount Sterling
(5,842 feet)

Mount Sterling Trail

Mount Sterling Gap

Old NC 284

Correll Branch

Mt. Sterling Ridge Trail

Dude Branch

0   ½   1
MILES

2.3. The trail has now climbed 1,600 feet. Turn right at the junction, staying on the Mount Sterling Trail. Hike through forested and grassy areas, then pass a horse-hitch rack just before arriving at the top of Mount Sterling at mile 2.8. The mountaintop is also the location of the Mount Sterling backcountry campsite, #38.

The tower is at the crest of the mountain. Baxter Creek trail, which comes from the Big Creek Ranger Station, also ends at the tower. If you are thirsty, a spring can be found on a side trail to your left, a half-mile down the Baxter Creek Trail. The park's eastern edge is the featured view from the tower. The main crest of the Smokies lies to the north. To the east, I-40 cuts through the Pigeon River gorge. In the summer, the grassy area below the tower is an ideal lunch spot.

Directions: From I-40, take the Waterville exit, #451. Cross the Pigeon River, then turn left to follow it upstream. At a point 2.3 miles after crossing the Pigeon, turn left on old NC 284 at Mount Sterling Village. Follow the dirt road 7 miles to Mount Sterling Gap. The Mount Sterling Trail starts on your right at the gap.

Little Cataloochee Church

Scenery:	★★★★	Difficulty:	★★
Trail Conditions:	★★★★	Solitude:	★★★★★
Children:	★★★★		

Distance: 7.6 miles round-trip
Hiking Time: 3:45 round-trip
Outstanding Features: multiple historic homesites, Little
Cataloochee Church

The hike to Little Cataloochee Church is an historic trip to a mountain valley setting left over from the last century. Starting on Pretty Hollow Gap Trail, you'll hike past old fields and evidence of settlement before turning on the Little Cataloochee Trail. Then you'll climb to Davidson Gap and into the Little Cataloochee valley, with its many old homesites, to finally end up at Little Cataloochee Church. This fine structure was built in 1890 and is maintained to this day.

Leave Cataloochee Road and pass the Cataloochee horse camp at mile 0.2. Hike by some old fields, known as Indian Flats, so named because Indians were there when the pioneers first set foot up this watershed. Come to the Little Cataloochee Trail junction at mile 0.7. Bear right on the Little Cataloochee Trail on an old roadbed, heading for Davidson Gap along Davidson Branch, which you'll cross several times.

Veer right up a tributary of Davidson Branch at mile 1.7. The trail steepens considerably, passing the remains of a settler's cabin on the left before reaching Davidson Gap at mile 2.3. Descend into the Little Cataloochee valley, where more settlements were strung along Little Cataloochee Creek and its tributaries.

One tributary, Coggins Branch, will lead you into the valley. Of course, it has homesites of its own, marked by fence posts, rock walls and old foundations, the most prominent of which is the Dan Cook place at mile 3.0. Built in 1856, the main house is deteriorating in the moist mountain climate, but the stone remnants of the barn remain intact.

Pass more reminders of human's presence, coming to Little Cataloochee Baptist Church at mile 3.8. After

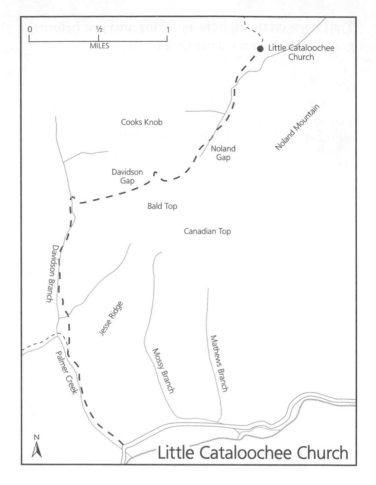

Little Cataloochee Church

passing so many dilapidated remains, the well-maintained white church looks even more impressive. An accompanying graveyard lies nearby. Local families keep the church up.

The church makes a great base for further exploration of the entire valley and all its historic settlements. Remember that the remains are a living archaeological exhibit of life in the Smokies and artifacts should be left where they are found. Enjoy this hike into history in the Little Cataloochee valley.

Directions: Leave I-40 at exit 20 to NC 276. Follow it a short distance and turn right on Cove Creek Road, which you follow nearly 6 miles to enter the park. Two miles inside the park, turn left onto Cataloochee Road. Follow it until it becomes gravel. The Pretty Hollow Gap

Trail starts on the right in a parking area just before the gravel road crosses Palmer Creek.

Cabin Flats via Bradley Fork

Scenery: ★★★★ Difficulty: ★★
Trail Conditions: ★★★★★ Solitude: ★★★
Children: ★★★★
Distance: 10.4 miles round-trip
Hiking Time: 5:15 round-trip
Outstanding Features: Bradley Fork, big trees

The hike to Cabin Flats is one of those deep forest ventures that shows its beauty in countless little ways, as opposed to a hike to a vista. The Bradley Fork Trail climbs very gradually on an old jeep road, allowing the hiker to admire Bradley Fork, an archetypal Smoky Mountain stream, as it works its way down to Smokemont amid a forest replete with native flora.

Bradley Fork Trail leaves the Smokemont campground, with Bradley Fork on the left. Pass a side road leading to the water supply for Smokemont campground at mile 0.3. Buildings and houses once occupied both sides of Bradley Fork; look for level areas with thin forest cover. Cross a wooden bridge over Chasteen Creek at mile 1.0. Just beyond this crossing is the Chasteen Creek Trail junction. Above this small clearing is the Lower Chasteen Creek backcountry campsite, #50.

Continuing on the Bradley Fork Trail, you come to the Smokemont Loop Trail junction at mile 1.6., then to a horse rail beside a nearby cascade at mile 2.5. The Bradley Fork Trail then crosses an island on Bradley Fork at mile 3.1, by means of two wide bridges. Cross Tabor Branch, then Bradley Fork again, just as Taywa Creek spills in from the right at mile 3.6.

Follow the jeep road a half-mile farther to the Cabin Flats Trail junction at mile 4.1. Go forward on the Cabin Flats Trail and immediately cross Bradley Fork on an impressive trestle bridge that seems oddly out of place in these old growth woods. Cross Tennessee Branch on a footbridge, just before the Dry Sluice Gap Trail junction at mile 4.6.

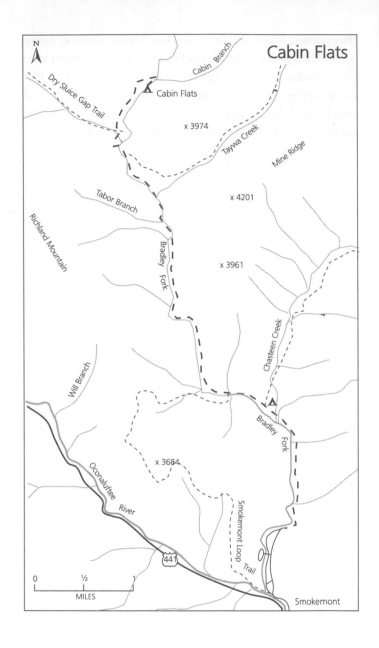

Cabin Flats

The Cabin Flats Trail winds along the west side of the Bradley Fork valley before descending into Cabin Flats proper, at mile 5.2, after a sharp right turn. This is the location of the Cabin Flats backcountry campsite, #49. The lower end of the campsite offers a nice pool for cooling off. Just below the pool is a massive log jam, a relic of the spring flood of 1994.

Directions: From the Oconaluftee Visitor Center, drive 3.2 miles north on Newfound Gap Road. Turn right into the Smokemont campground on a bridge over the Oconaluftee River. Veer left and pass the campground check-in station. The Bradley Fork Trail starts at the gated jeep road at the right rear of the campground.

Kephart Shelter via Kephart Prong

Scenery:	★★★★	Difficulty:	★
Trail Conditions:	★★★★★	Solitude:	★★★
Children:	★★★★★		

Distance: 4.0 miles round-trip
Hiking Time: 2:00 round-trip
Outstanding Features: mountain stream, old Civilian
Conservation Corps camp

This hike exemplifies the effects people have had on the Smokies and the truly amazing powers nature has to recuperate from such influence. After crossing the Oconaluftee River, you'll enter a former Civilian Conservation Corps camp, a relic of the New Deal era of the 1930s. Next is the site of an early park service fish hatchery. Follow the course of Kephart Prong to a backcountry shelter in an old lumber camp. The dry shelter that awaits at journey's end could make this a favorable rainy day hike.

Start the hike by crossing the Oconaluftee River on a wide bridge. At mile 0.2, enter the former CCC camp. Pieces of paving, a large chimney, building foundations, scattered tools and even an old water fountain remain in the second-growth woodland. Explore the area and see what other signs you can spot of the lives of these young men.

Veer left beyond the camp and cross Kephart Prong on a footlog at mile 0.3. This footlog, like many others in the park, has a thin veneer of moss and can be slippery in the damp climate of the Smokies. Turn right and trace Kephart Prong. Up ahead is the former fish hatchery. Look around for signs of people's attempt to amend the ravages of negligent logging practices before the establishment of the national park. Logging silted

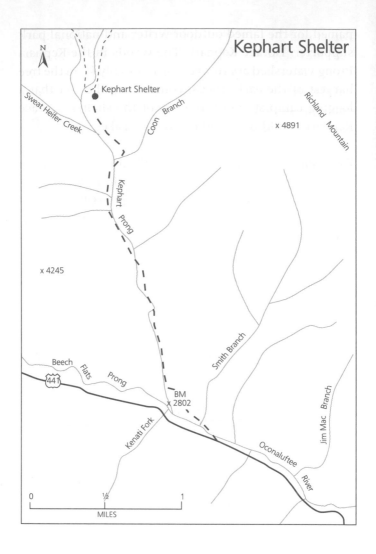

Kephart Shelter

streams, killing fish native to the Smokies; hence the fish hatchery.

Cross Kephart Prong on a footlog at mile 0.7 and again at mile 1.0. Be careful to watch for the footlog crossings; they may be up or downstream of where the trail crosses the creek. Kephart Prong Trail is a horse and hiking trail, and horses of course do not use the footbridges, making their own trail directly across the creek.

Rejoin the railroad grade, then cross the stream on a fourth footlog at mile 1.5. Continue on the right side of Kephart Prong to arrive at the Kephart shelter at mile 2.0. The stream, shelter and nearby Mount Kephart are named for the famed outdoor writer and national park supporter, Horace Kephart. The woods in the Kephart Prong watershed are recovering admirably from the tree harvest of the early 1900s, considering the fact that a logging camp stood on the site of the shelter. Horace Kephart would be proud of his namesake.

Directions: From the Sugarlands Visitors Center, drive south 8.8 miles beyond Newfound Gap into North Carolina on Newfound Gap Road. The Kephart Prong Trail is on your left. From the Oconaluftee Visitor Center, drive 6.8 miles north on Newfound Gap Road. The Kephart Prong Trail is on your right.

Bone Valley via Fontana Lake

Scenery:	★★★★★	Difficulty:	★★
Trail Conditions:	★★★★	Solitude:	★★★
Children:	★★★		

Distance: 13.8 miles round-trip
Hiking Time: 6:45 round-trip
Outstanding Features: Fontana Lake, Hazel Creek, clearing at Bone Valley

The trip to Bone Valley requires a little planning, but it will offer a view of the Smokies you can't get any other way. From Fontana Village Marina, ride a shuttle boat eastward along Fontana Lake, product of the dammed Little Tennessee River, whose northern shoreline is the Great Smoky Mountains National Park. (To arrange for your shuttle, call Fontana Marina at (704) 498-2211, extension 277. The friendly staff will boat you to Hazel Creek and arrange a time for your return shuttle.) Boat north into the Hazel Creek embayment and land near the old town site of Proctor, where Hazel Creek flows into Fontana Lake. Make the hike along historic Hazel Creek, the site of pioneer activity from the 1830s to the 1940s, up to Bone Valley and a clearing, location of Hall Cabin. The trail from Fontana Lake to Bone Valley gains a moderate 100 feet per mile, making the hike easier than the distance suggests.

As you leave the marina, Shuckstack fire tower

stands tall to the northwest, the Eagle Creek embayment to the north. Enter the Hazel Creek embayment and begin your hike on the Lakeshore Trail. Head north along Hazel Creek, coming to the Proctor Creek backcountry campsite, #86, at mile 0.5. Shortly beyond the Proctor campsite, cross Hazel Creek on a wide bridge. The white house by the creek is used by park personnel. Pass the Proctor cemetery on your left at mile 1.2. Many logging and homestead artifacts can be seen from the trail as you hike along Hazel Creek. Span two more wide bridges before arriving at the Sawdust Pile backcountry campsite, #85, at mile 3.3.

Continue along Hazel Creek, crossing the creek on two more bridges to arrive at the Sugar Fork backcountry campsite, #84, and a trail junction, at mile 4.5. The Lakeshore Trail leads left; keep hiking forward, crossing the wooden bridge on the Hazel Creek Trail. The trail climbs above the creek to intersect the Bone Valley Trail junction at mile 5.2.

Turn left up the Bone Valley Trail and ford Bone Valley Creek three times in the next mile. Old farm sites are evident through this section. Make a fourth ford,

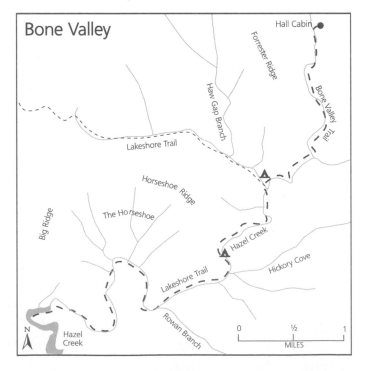

then arrive at Hall Cabin at mile 6.9. In the pleasant clearing near the cabin lie the remains of a hunting lodge. A small side trail to the left of the cabin leads to the Hall Cemetery. When the air and water are warm, you can stretch your explorations over a long summer's day, making this an ideal all-day trip.

Directions: From Townsend, Tennessee, take US 321 north to the Foothills Parkway. Follow Foothills Parkway west to US 129. Turn south on US 129 into North Carolina. Turn left on NC 28 passing Fontana Village. 1.5 miles past Fontana Village entrance, turn left at the sign to Fontana Dam. Then turn right at the sign to Fontana Village Marina, a short distance away. From Bryson City, North Carolina, take US 19 south to NC 28. Follow NC 28 for nearly 25 miles to turn right at the sign to Fontana Dam, then right to Fontana Village Marina.

Shuckstack from Twentymile Ranger Station

Scenery:	★★★★★	Difficulty:	★★★
Trail Conditions:	★★★★★	Solitude:	★★★★
Children:	★★		
Distance: 10.2 miles round-trip			
Hiking Time: 5:15 round-trip			
Outstanding Features: waterfall, views from Shuckstack Mountain			

Twentymile is one of the Smokies' most remote areas. You'll travel along Twentymile Creek on an old railroad grade, past Twentymile Cascades, up to the Appalachian Trail and Shuckstack Mountain, to a fire tower that offers one of those worth-the-effort, above-the-treetops, 360-degree panoramas.

Begin your hike at the gated road on the Twentymile Trail. This trail is rockier than it was before the spring flood of '94. Pass a park service barn in a clearing on your right. Cross Moore Spring Branch on a wide bridge at mile 0.6. On the far side of the bridge is the Wolf

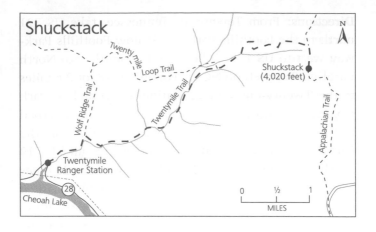

Ridge Trail junction. Bear right, staying on the Twentymile Trail. At mile 0.7, a sign marks the side trail to the bottom of Twentymile Cascades. Take the side trail for a view of the creek dropping over a series of wide stone slabs.

Return to the main trail, gradually ascending. Cross Twentymile Creek on wide bridges at mile 1.4 and 1.6. Come to the Twentymile Creek backcountry campsite, #93, at mile 1.7. Immediately cross another bridge beyond the campsite. The trail now runs farther above the creek, passing over tributary streams, only to cross Twentymile Creek twice more on bridges before arriving at Proctor Gap and a trail junction at mile 3.0.

Bear right at the trail junction, staying on the Twentymile Trail and its steady grade, the trail now paralleling Proctor Branch. At mile 3.5, the trail steepens, leaving Proctor Branch behind. The final ascent to the A.T. is completed in a series of switchbacks to arrive at Sassafras Gap at mile 4.7.

Turn right on the A.T., climbing out of Sassafras Gap, and come to a side trail on top of Shuckstack at mile 5.0. Turn left and climb a steep grade 0.1 mile to the top of Shuckstack and a fire tower (elevation 4,020 feet). Atop the tower, views abound. To the north and northeast runs the main crest of the Smokies. Fontana Lake covers the flooded valley of the Little Tennessee River to the southeast. From this vantage point, the surrounding southern Appalachian sea of mountains looks especially rugged.

Directions: From Townsend, Tennessee, take US 321 north to the Foothills Parkway. Follow Foothills Parkway west to US 129. Follow US 129 south into North Carolina. Turn left on NC 28. Follow NC 28 for 2.6 miles to the Twentymile Ranger Station, on your left. Park beyond the ranger station and walk up to the gated road to begin your hike on the Twentymile Trail. From the courthouse in Bryson City, North Carolina, take US 19 south for 5.4 miles to NC 28. Follow NC 28 for 30 miles to reach the Twentymile Ranger Station, which will be on your right.

Part II:
Great Day Loops

▲▲▲

Loops of Tennessee

Pine Mountain Loop

Scenery:	★★★★	Difficulty:	★★★
Trail Conditions:	★★★★	Solitude:	★★★★
Children:	★★★		

Distance: 7.9 miles round-trip
Hiking Time: 4:00 round-trip
Outstanding Features: pine-oak forest, Abrams Creek

The two ford crossings of Abrams Creek account for the difficulty rating of this hike. The first ford might be avoided, especially during the summer months when the footlog is restored after winter rains. The second ford is the toughest in the park. But don't let the fords discourage you from taking this scenic loop hike. It is a good opportunity to explore the pine-oak forested western end of the park in a less peopled setting. You'll leave Abrams Creek Ranger Station to cross Abrams the first time. Then wind up Pine Mountain on a jeep road, descending into Scott Gap. Next, work your way down a south slope to cross Abrams Creek again. Follow Abrams Creek on the narrow twisting Little Bottoms Trail, to return to the ranger station via Cooper Road.

Start your hike by walking back toward the Abrams Creek Ranger Station from the parking area. The Rabbit Creek Trail starts at the upper end of the horse pasture. Follow the Rabbit Creek Trail to the first crossing of Abrams Creek at 0.1 mile. Look downstream for the footlog. If it's not there, you'll have to ford the creek.

After crossing Abrams, immediately enter an old homesite, with reforesting fields and an old chimney. Start the climb up Pine Mountain, switching back at the point of a ridge. Top out on Pine Mountain at mile 2.0, then descend to Scott Gap and a trail junction at mile 2.5.

Near the gap is the Scott Gap trail shelter and a spring to your right. Turn left at the gap on the Hannah Mountain Trail. The trail follows south slopes on its decline to Abrams Creek, with many laurel bushes and pine trees along the route. The second Abrams Creek crossing is at mile 4.3. This is a ford for sure. Find a stout limb for balance and face upstream as you ford.

Once across, you'll come to Hatcher Mountain Trail junction. Turn left on the Hatcher Mountain Trail and climb a short distance to another trail junction at mile 4.5. Turn left again and follow the Little Bottoms Trail, which winds far above the Abrams Creek gorge, only to drop down to creek level at the Little Bottoms backcountry campsite, #17, at mile 5.3.

The trail snakes along the creek, then leaves the

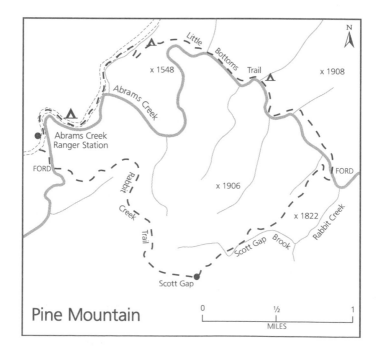

gorge to top a side ridge at mile 6.5. A couple of switchbacks and you'll be down at Kingfisher Creek and the Cooper Road Trail junction at mile 6.8. Turn left on Cooper Road Trail to arrive at the Abrams Creek campground at mile 7.9. The parking area is 0.5 mile further down Abrams Creek Road.

Directions: From Townsend, Tennessee drive north on US 321. Turn left onto the Foothills Parkway, then left again 18 miles later onto US 129 at Chilhowee Lake. Head south 0.5 mile to Happy Valley Road. Turn left on Happy Valley Road, following it 6 miles to Abrams Creek Road. Turn right on Abrams Creek Road and drive 1 mile to the campground, passing the ranger station. Cooper Road Trail starts at the rear of the campground. Park your car in the designated area near the ranger station.

Rich Mountain Loop

Scenery:	★★★★	Difficulty:	★★
Trail Conditions:	★★★★★	Solitude:	★★★
Children:	★★★		
Distance: 8.5 miles round-trip			
Hiking Time: 4:15 round-trip			
Outstanding Features: old cabin, view of Cades Cove and mountains beyond			

This is a good day hike that shows Cades Cove from a different perspective, with a stop by the historic John Oliver cabin thrown in for good measure. Initially you'll stay in the basin of the cove, then climb up Rich Mountain to an inspiring overlook. After you top out on Rich Mountain, with good but interspersed views, you'll circle back down on the Crooked Arm Ridge Trail, completing the loop.

Start your hike on the Rich Mountain Loop Trail, rock hopping over Crooked Arm Branch, then come to a trail junction at mile 0.5. This is the return point of your loop. Veer left on the Rich Mountain Loop Trail. Cross Harrison Branch as you keep a northwesterly course. At mile 1.2, the John Oliver cabin, built in 1820, will be on your left. Oliver was an early settler of the

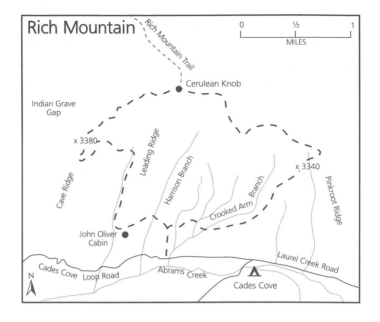

Rich Mountain

Indian Grave Gap

Cerulean Knob

Rich Mountain Trail

x 3380

Leading Ridge

Harrison Branch

Cave Ridge

John Oliver Cabin

Crooked Arm Branch

x 3340

Pinkroot Ridge

Laurel Creek Road

Cades Cove Loop Road

Abrams Creek

Cades Cove

0   ½   1
MILES

N

cove and helped populate it with his many offspring.

The climb begins in earnest when you turn up Martha's Branch and begin switchbacking up Rich Mountain, along Cave Ridge. Your first notable view of the cove opens up on your left at mile 3.0, just as you come to the 3,000-foot level. The Indian Grave Gap Trail junction is at mile 3.4 and offers another cove view.

Turn right and begin moderately climbing on the Indian Grave Gap Trail, reaching the Rich Mountain Trail junction at mile 4.2. Push on up the Indian Grave Gap Trail near the top of Rich Mountain, where a fire tower once stood near the spur trail to your left. The forest cover limits the views now, but the clearing makes an ideal picnic spot.

Start descending down Rich Mountain. At mile 5.9, near a clearing for a power line, is a trail junction for Crooked Arm Ridge Trail. As you begin the trail, keep your eyes up to see the vista from an overlook. Switchback down towards Cades Cove, crossing Crooked Arm Branch near the base of the mountain.

Complete the loop at mile 8.0, when the trail intersects the Rich Mountain Loop Trail. Follow it 0.5 mile back down to the loop road and the cove you just viewed from above.

Directions: From Townsend, Tennessee, drive east on US 321. From the Townsend "Y" go 5.6 miles and turn right onto Laurel Creek Road and follow it for 7.4 miles to the beginning of Cades Cove Loop Road. Park at the beginning of the loop and walk a short ways down the loop road to the Rich Mountain Loop trail, which is on your right.

Spence Field-Russell Field Loop

Scenery:	★★★★★	Difficulty:	★★★
Trail Conditions:	★★★★	Solitude:	★★★
Children:	★★		

Distance: 12.9 miles
Hiking Time: 6:45
Outstanding Features: Spence Field, Little Bald, Russell Field

    This strenuous all-day hike provides ample reward for those who want to see the Smokies from bottom to top. Starting in Cades Cove, you will climb along a deeply forested, crashing mountain stream to ultimately intersect with the main crest of the Smokies and the famed Appalachian Trail. Once you're on the A.T., outstanding views lie before you at Spence Field and Little Bald. Return to Cades Cove via Russell Field Trail with its section of old growth trees.

    Follow the Anthony Creek Trail beyond the horse camp and intersect Crib Gap Trail at mile 0.5. Continue straight and make the first of four crossings of Anthony Creek and its tributaries. The bigger crossings offer footbridges for ease of travel. Just beyond the fourth creek crossing, come to a trail junction at mile 1.3. You'll return here when you complete the loop. Follow the Anthony Creek Trail on the left, saving the Russell Field Trail for the return journey. Continuing to climb, the trail passes the Anthony Creek backcountry campsite, #9, to your right, at mile 2.6. Shortly beyond the campsite, you'll leave Anthony Creek and intersect the Bote Mountain Trail at mile 3.2. Turn right up the Bote Mountain Trail and head up along the old jeep road to a turnaround at mile 3.9. The trail narrows and becomes a

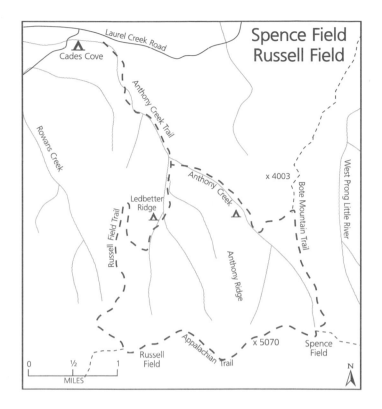

deeply rutted rocky path that ascends steadily through rhododendron to arrive at the lower reaches of Spence Field and the A.T. at mile 5.5.

Take time to explore this former pasture that offers grand views of Fontana Lake in North Carolina and Cades Cove in Tennessee. It is an ideal spot to have a snack and rest before you turn west on the A.T. toward Russell Field. In Spence Field, the A.T. passes the Eagle Creek Trail, where a backcountry shelter and spring are located at the meadow's southern edge.

Leave Spence Field on the A.T. and reenter the woods. At mile 6.6 of your loop hike, come to Little Bald, a more favorable location for those seeking solitude. The field is being overtaken by trees but still offers good views into the Carolina side of the park and beyond. The trail descends for the most part to Russell Field and another trail shelter at mile 8.2. Just in front of the shelter is a trail junction and your departure from the A.T. Turn right on the Russell Field Trail and pass a spring before entering Russell Field. Today, the field is surrounded by forest but remains special despite the lack of views. You can't help but sense the serenity of this highland meadow.

Descend upon entering the forest, which eventually changes to pine-oak on the easy-walking Ledbetter Ridge the trail follows. At mile 10.0, leave Ledbetter Ridge and reenter the Anthony Creek watershed. Between the ridge and Ledbetter Ridge backcountry campsite, #10, at mile 10.8, pass through an old growth forest of primarily hemlocks and tulip trees. At mile 11.6, you'll return to the intersection with the Anthony Creek Trail. Retrace your steps down the Anthony Creek Trail to arrive at the Cades Cove picnic area at mile 12.9.

Directions: Just before the beginning of the Cades Cove Loop Road, turn left toward the campground, then turn left into the picnic area. The Anthony Creek Trail is on your right at the back of the picnic area. Find the trailhead and return toward the campground. Park your car in the lot beside the ranger station.

Finley Cane Loop

Scenery:	★★★★	Difficulty:	★★
Trail Conditions:	★★★★	Solitude:	★★★★
Children:	★★★★		

Distance: 8.9 miles round-trip
Hiking Time: 4:15 round-trip
Outstanding Features: old homesites, mountainsides
small creeks

Although you must cross a road during this excursion, the trails on this hike are lightly used, offering a pleasantly undulating loop with very little climbing for such a mountainous setting. First, you'll walk among old homesites, the trail gently winding along the side of Turkeypen Ridge, then you'll follow an old road to the historic Bote Mountain Trail. The Bote Mountain Trail will lead you to the Finley Cane Trail along the northern base of Bote Mountain to complete your loop.

Start your hike on the Turkeypen Ridge Trail, descending from Big Spring Cove into the Crib Gap Trail junction at mile 0.2. Continue on the Turkeypen Trail through an old homesite with relics scattered about amid sparse woods. Leave Big Spring Cove to work your way up to a nearly level ridge extending out from a flank of Scott Mountain. Drop slightly to cross the most notable creek on the path, Pinkroot Branch, at mile 1.3.

Wind your way along Turkeypen Ridge and notice the differing forest types, each dependent upon the amount of the sun's exposure on the land. South-facing slopes will include various species of pine and mountain laurel, whereas the shaded ravines support hemlock and rhododendron. The trail takes a northeasterly angle, sloping down to the Schoolhouse Gap Trail at mile 3.4.

Turn right on the Schoolhouse Gap Trail and follow it along Spence Branch to Laurel Creek Road at mile 4.5. Turn left on the road for 50 yards and cross over to the Bote Mountain Trail. Return to the woods up this former road. Along with the Schoolhouse Gap road-turned-trail, this trail was once part of a scheme to connect Maryville, Tennessee, to the Hazel Creek area.

Stay on the Bote Mountain Trail as you pass the West Prong Trail at mile 5.7. On your right, at mile 6.3,

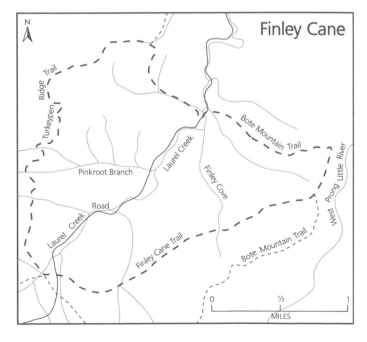

your loop, the Finley Cane Trail. Turn
ey Cane Trail, with its northern expo-
ands featuring tulip trees, sugar maple,
eech. Pass Finley Cane's only patch of
any small rills running perpendicular
to the trail, you'll rise in and out of watery hollows to a
trail junction at mile 8.3. To the right, a horse trail passes
under Laurel Creek Road to connect with the Turkeypen
Ridge Trail. Continue forward on the Finley Cane Trail
to complete your loop to Laurel Creek Road and the Big
Spring Cove parking area at mile 8.9.

Directions: From Townsend, Tennessee, drive east 5.6
miles, turning left at the Townsend "Y" onto Laurel
Creek Road towards Cades Cove. The Turkeypen Ridge
Trail is on your right at the small Big Spring Cove parking area that extends on both sides of the road.

▲▲▲

Loops of North Carolina

Boogerman Loop

Scenery:	★★★★★	Difficulty:	★★★
Trail Conditions:	★★★★	Solitude:	★★★★
Children:	★★★		

Distance: 7.4 miles round-trip
Hiking Time: 3:15 round-trip
Outstanding Features: old homesites, huge hemlocks,
white pines, tulip trees

A footlog crossing is an appropriate beginning for
this hike; you'll be quite familiar with them before this
loop is over. But first, enjoy the beauty of huge trees,
old homesites and mountain streams on this fulfilling
hike, whose trail name was the nickname of the man
who owned the land, one Robert "Boogerman" Palmer.
There is quite a bit of up and down, but the trail mak-

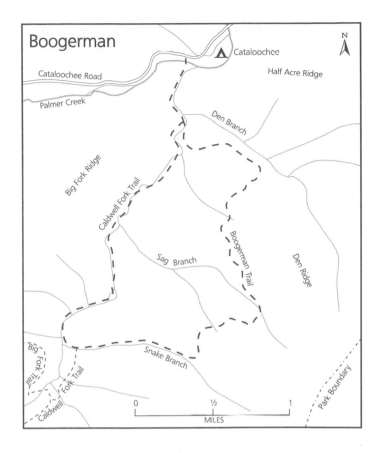

ers, while using old roads, made a few twists and turns to take you by the biggest trees in the area.

Cross Cataloochee Creek on a footbridge and enter a stand of white pines. Soon the trail splits; stay right and climb a narrow edge along Caldwell Fork. Descend and soon come to the north end of the Boogerman Loop Trail at mile 0.8. Turn left, crossing Caldwell Fork on a footbridge and entering an area of old growth trees. Leave the cove and climb along a dry ridge. Pass through a gap, and white pines dominate the down slope to the Boogerman's homestead at mile 2.8.

Hike away from the homestead and wind through a series of coves, where the trail intentionally nears many old tulip trees. If you look carefully, you'll notice the tops have been sheared off most of these giants—the result of hundreds of years of rough living in the Smokies. At the last gap, the trail drops straight down and doubles as a streambed in wet weather. At mile 3.8

of your loop, the trail veers right down along Snake Branch, around a rock wall, then fords the small stream. Clearings, old fences and piles of stone are other indicators of homesites along this creek.

More white pines signal your arrival at the Caldwell Fork Trail junction at mile 4.6. Turn right and head down this picturesque valley. Cross Snake Branch on a footlog and soon start the nine footbridge crossings of Caldwell Fork amid the towering hemlocks. The Caldwell Fork Trail can be muddy and confusing; at stream crossings, the trail frequently splits. Hikers go one way over footbridges and horses ford the creek. Always take the trail headed for higher, drier ground.

These footbridges are a way to appreciate without getting wet the normally crystal clear creek as you descend the valley, with its alternating deep pools and clamoring falls and riffles. At mile 6.6, come again to the northern junction of the Boogerman Loop Trail. Continue down the Caldwell Fork Trail, again passing the needle-carpeted area of white pines. The crossing of Cataloochee Creek on a footbridge at mile 7.4 signals the completion of the loop.

Directions: Leave I-40 at exit 20 and drive west on NC 276. Follow it a short distance, then turn right onto Cove Creek Road, which you follow nearly 6 miles to enter the park. Two miles beyond the park boundary, turn left onto the paved Cataloochee Road. Follow it 3.1 miles. The Caldwell Fork Trail and its footbridge over Cataloochee Creek will be on your left.

Hyatt Ridge Loop

Scenery:	★★★★	Difficulty:	★★★
Trail Conditions:	★★★★	Solitude:	★★★★★
Children:	★★★		

Distance: 7.8 miles round-trip
Hiking Time: 4:15 round-trip
Outstanding Features: isolation, old growth forest

This loop hike takes you away from Straight Fork Road into the seldom visited high country on Hyatt Ridge. Take the side trail to the McGhee Spring backcountry campsite for lunch (this adds 1.8 miles to the hike), then return via the Beech Gap Trail to Straight Fork. A short walk along the lightly used Straight Fork Road will complete your loop.

Start your trip on the Hyatt Ridge Trail, beyond the gate on an old railroad grade, crossing Hyatt Creek at mile 0.7. Continue to ascend steeply through second growth forest up the side of Hyatt Ridge. Come to Low Gap and a trail junction atop Hyatt Ridge (elevation 4,400 feet) at mile 1.9. Straight ahead is the Enloe Creek Trail. A lot of spruce grow on this ridge.

Turn right, staying on the Hyatt Ridge Trail. Climb out of the gap for another 0.5 mile and come to an area of old growth forest. Veer left, then make a sharp right turn, climbing northeasterly on Hyatt Bald, now wooded with a grassy understory, a reminder of its former state.

At mile 3.6, you come to another trail junction. This 0.9-mile trail leads to the McGhee Spring backcountry campsite, #44 (elevation 5,040 feet), an excellent lunch spot located by a perennial spring in a mountain glade. To continue the Hyatt Ridge Loop, turn right on the Beech Gap Trail (once known as the Hyatt Bald Trail). Sections of this trail have tall, waving grasses under the trees.

Descend gradually on the Beech Gap Trail, maintaining a northeasterly course. At mile 4.4, in a grassy gap, make a switchback to the right, leaving the ridge top. Wind your way southward, passing the upper reaches of Grass Branch at mile 5.4. Soon the waters of

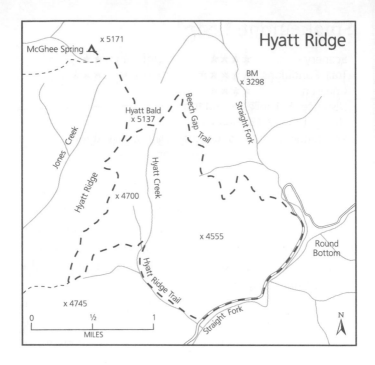

Straight Fork hum in the distance, as the trail skirts more small branches, to arrive at Straight Fork Road, at mile 6.5.

Turn right on Straight Fork Road, following its namesake stream down into Big Cove and Cherokee Reservation territory. This lightly used road actually makes for pleasant walking. An occasional fisherman may be encountered along the stream. Arrive at the Hyatt Ridge trailhead on your right at mile 7.8 to complete the loop.

Directions: From Oconaluftee Visitor Center, drive 1 mile south to Big Cove Road. Turn left on Big Cove Road and follow it 10.4 miles to the park boundary. Drive 2.5 miles beyond the boundary to the Hyatt Ridge trailhead, which will be on your left.

Smokemont Loop

Scenery:	★★★★	Difficulty:	★★
Trail Conditions:	★★★★★	Solitude:	★★★
Children:	★★★★		

Distance: 5.4 miles round-trip
Hiking Time: 2:45 round-trip
Outstanding Features: good family day hike through
history and woods

This loop hike leads away from the popular Smokemont campground, along Bradley Fork, then upward along the southern reaches of Richland Mountain. The trail winds back down near the Oconaluftee River, past the Bradley Cemetery, returning to the Smokemont campground.

Start your loop hike on the Bradley Fork Trail, at the rear of the Smokemont campground. Pass an outbuilding, then a side road on your right leading to the water supply for the campground at mile 0.3. Open areas with thin forest cover indicate former homesites along the trail. At mile 1.0, cross a wide wooden bridge over Chasteen Creek, then come to the Chasteen Creek

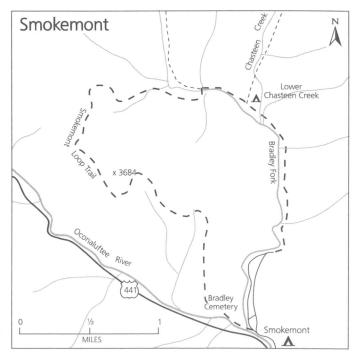

Smokemont

N

Chasteen Creek

Lower
Chasteen Creek

Bradley Fork

Smokemont Loop Trail

x 3684

Oconaluftee River

441

Bradley
Cemetery

Smokemont

0   ½   1
MILES

Trail junction. Press forward through the junction and come to the Smokemont Loop Trail junction at mile 1.6.

Turn left on the Smokemont Loop Trail, crossing Bradley Fork on a long footbridge, then a smaller branch on another footbridge. The narrow foot trail immediately switchbacks right, then left, swings around a knob on the way up Richland Mountain, reaching the crest at mile 2.7. The white noise of the Oconaluftee River accompanies you on your southward journey along Richland Mountain.

The trail reaches its high point, nearly 3,500 feet, at mile 3.4. A couple of downed logs invite a rest. The trail begins to wind down the slope of Richland Mountain, alternately flanked by open woods and thick rhododendron. At mile 5.0, the Bradley Cemetery appears on your right, downtrail. Continue down to a jeep road that used to loop through a now closed section of the Smokemont campground, and turn right to reach a side trail to the cemetery. Climb a small hill to the cemetery. Worn-down stones that mark graves of settlers whose names are lost to time stand beside graves marked with readable names.

Return to the jeep road and follow the road over Bradley Fork on an old stone bridge back to the Smokemont campground at mile 5.4, completing your loop. The Bradley Fork trailhead is up to your left at the rear of the campground.

Directions: From the Oconaluftee Visitor Center, drive 3.2 miles north on Newfound Gap Road. Turn right into the Smokemont campground on a bridge over the Oconaluftee River. Veer left and pass the campground check-in station. The Bradley Fork Trail starts at the gated jeep road at the right rear of the campground.

Indian Creek Loop

Scenery: ★★★★   Difficulty: ★★★
Trail Conditions: ★★★★   Solitude: ★★★
Children: ★★★
Distance: 12.4 miles round-trip
Hiking Time: 6:15 round-trip
Outstanding Features: quiet ridge, Indian Creek Falls

This loop hike follows Deep Creek to Indian Creek, past Indian Creek Falls, then climbs to Martins Gap. You return via the quiet Sunkota Ridge Trail with its drier-type forest, back to Deep Creek and its accompanying riverine habitat. The biological diversity of the Smokies can be well appreciated on this fairly easy trek through the relatively small area.

Start your hike on the Deep Creek Trail at the end of Deep Creek Road just beyond the Deep Creek campground. Follow an old gravel road, crossing Deep Creek on a bridge en route to the Indian Creek Trail junction, at mile 0.7. Turn right on the Indian Creek Trail, coming to Indian Creek Falls at mile 0.8. A short side trail on your right leads to the base of the falls. At mile 1.2, the Stone Pile Gap Trail leaves to your right. Then, at mile 1.5, the Loop Trail heads up Sunkota Ridge to your left. Stay north on the Indian Creek Trail.

A number of pioneer homesites appear on the creek sides between several bridged crossings of Indian Creek. A gradual climb leads to the Deeplow Gap Trail junction at mile 3.6. Continue following the Indian Creek Trail to its end at mile 4.6, located at a road turnaround near Estes Branch. The park service arbitrarily starts the Martins Gap Trail at this point.

Keep hiking through the turnaround, and begin the Martins Gap Trail. Within the next half-mile, you'll cross Indian Creek three times on footbridges before switchbacking up the side of Sunkota Ridge to arrive at Martins Gap at mile 6.4. Martins Gap, a sag on Sunkota Ridge, has a four-way trail intersection. Turn left on the serene Sunkota Ridge Trail. Sunkota is the pioneer interpretation of the Indian word meaning apple.

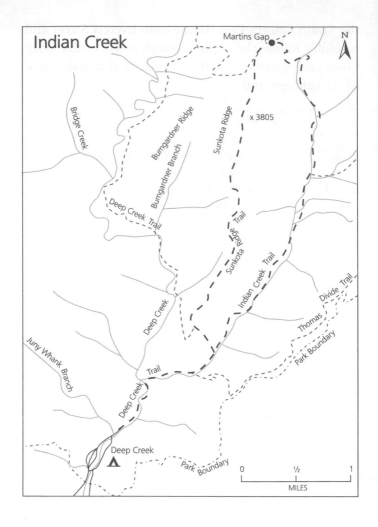

Climb out of the gap to the loop's high point at mile 7.2, and begin a slow descent, winding along the ridge top and its flanks. At mile 10.2, come to the end of the Sunkota Ridge Trail and the Loop Trail junction. Turn right on the Loop Trail down to the Deep Creek Trail at mile 10.7. Follow Deep Creek Trail downstream over three bridges to the Indian Creek Trail at mile 11.7. Return to the trailhead on the short section of the Deep Creek Trail you traversed earlier to the Deep Creek trailhead at mile 12.4.

Directions: From the Oconaluftee Visitor Center, take US 441 south to Cherokee, North Carolina. Turn right on US 19 to Bryson City, North Carolina. Turn right at the Swain County Courthouse onto Everett Street and carefully follow the signs through town to the Deep Creek campground. The Deep Creek Trail is at the back of the campground.

Goldmine Loop

Scenery: ★★★★   Difficulty: ★
Trail Conditions: ★★★★   Solitude: ★★★★★
Children: ★★★★★
Distance: 3.3 miles round-trip
Hiking Time: 1:45 round-trip
Outstanding Features: Fontana Lake, Lakeview tunnel, homesites

This short loop hike travels a seldom trod area of the Smokies. Beginning at Lakeview Drive, you hike down to Fontana Lake. The trail moves away from the lake, passing several old homesites along the way, then returns to Lakeview Road through the Lakeview tunnel. Several old roads and trails spur off the Goldmine loop, so watch your direction.

The loop hike starts near the parking area at the end of Lakeview Drive. With your back to the parking area, begin your hike on the Tunnel Bypass Trail across the road and to the left of the parking area. Once on the Tunnel Bypass Trail, descend briefly through a rhododendron thicket and then climb up to a small gap at mile 0.3. An old trail lies below and leads to the same gap. Proceed forward through the gap, skirting a knob to arrive at another gap and a trail junction on a modest ridge at mile 0.5.

Turn left on the Goldmine Loop Trail and descend down a ridge on the narrow path. Come to an old road that parallels Tunnel Branch and veer right. The forest is more closed in here than on the ridge top. The old road turns away from Tunnel Branch and comes to Fontana Lake at mile 1.3.

Intersect another road that swings around and over a tiny creek, then passes over Hyatt Branch via stone culverts. Come to the side trail leading to the Goldmine Branch backcountry campsite, #67, at mile 1.7. The

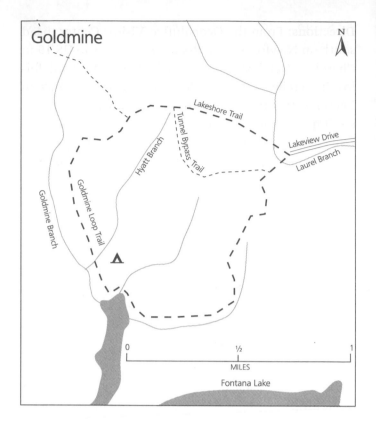

Goldmine

Lakeshore Trail

Tunnel Bypass Trail

Hyatt Branch

Lakeview Drive

Laurel Branch

Goldmine Loop Trail

Goldmine Branch

N

0   ½   1
MILES

Fontana Lake

campsite is located at an open homesite a few hundred yards up the side trail.

The Goldmine Loop Trail crosses Goldmine Branch again on a culvert, then becomes muddy. Beyond the muddy area, the trail briefly leaves the road and skirts to the right of a homesite to rejoin the old road to a second homesite at mile 2.2. A stone chimney stands near the trail. Swing past the homesite in a rhododendron tunnel to emerge at the top of the hollow. The road continues forward but the trail makes a sharp right up the side of a ridge to a saddle, then veers left for a short but steep climb to the Lakeshore Trail junction at mile 2.6.

Turn right on the Lakeshore Trail, and within a scant 100 yards, you'll come to the Tunnel Bypass Trail junction. Pass forward through the junction and come to the Lakeview tunnel at mile 2.9. Walk the 0.2-mile-long tunnel and emerge near the Lakeview Drive. Pass beyond the gate and complete your 3.3-mile loop.

Directions: From the Oconaluftee Visitor Center, head south on Newfound Gap Road for 3.2 miles to US 19 in Cherokee, North Carolina. Turn right on US 19 and follow it 10 miles to Bryson City, North Carolina. Once in Bryson City, turn right at the courthouse and continue straight on Everett Street, which becomes Lakeview Drive. The Lakeview Drive parking area is at the end of Lakeview Drive, 7.9 miles from the courthouse in Bryson City.

Twentymile Loop

Scenery:	★★★★	Difficulty:	★★
Trail Conditions:	★★★	Solitude:	★★★★★
Children:	★★★★		

Distance: 7.4 miles round-trip
Hiking Time: 3:45 round-trip
Outstanding Features: waterfall, mountain streams, deep woods

This streamside loop hike never gets too far from the sound of falling water, one of the key ingredients of the Smokies. This is one of the most rewarding out-of-the-way trips in the park. This hike travels along Twentymile Creek, then veers left on the Wolf Ridge Trail with Moore Spring Branch, a fine trout stream, as your noisy companion. Turn east on the Twentymile Loop Trail into deep woods, over Long Hungry Ridge down to the Twentymile Trail. Follow Twentymile Creek as it cascades down toward Cheoah Lake.

Start your loop on the Twentymile Trail, following it to mile 0.6, then hike over the bridged crossing of Moore Spring Branch to the Wolf Ridge Trail junction. Turn left on the Wolf Ridge Trail and cross Moore Spring Branch three times on footlogs in the first half-mile. Cross Moore Spring Branch without benefit of a footlog at mile 1.3 and 1.5.

At mile 1.6, at the Twentymile Loop Trail junction, turn right. The Twentymile Loop Trail heads east, fording Moore Spring Branch again, then ascends toward a gap. After some meandering up the side of Long Hungry Ridge, the trail passes through a sag in the ridge

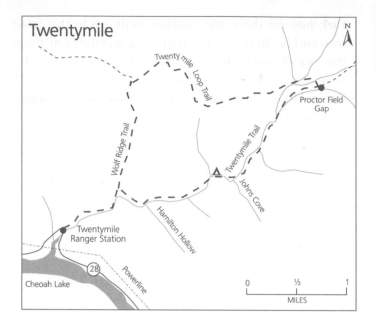

Proctor Field
Gap

Twenty mile Loop Trail

Wolf Ridge Trail

Twentymile Trail

Johns Cove

Hamilton Hollow

Twentymile
Ranger Station

28

Powerline

Cheoah Lake

N

0   ½   1
MILES

at mile 3.2, where a decomposing sign once announced the gap's name.

The Twentymile Loop Trail soon slopes sharply down heavily wooded Long Hungry Ridge, an ideal place to absorb the essence of the southern Appalachian forest. Ford Twentymile Creek at mile 4.2, then cross a level area to rise to Proctor Gap and a trail junction at mile 4.4.

Turn right on the Twentymile Trail, trailing Twentymile Creek downstream. Just after crossing a wide bridge, come to the Twentymile Creek backcountry campsite, #93, at mile 5.7. Cross two more bridges in short succession to arrive at the side trail for Twentymile Cascades, at mile 6.7. Take the side trail to view the waterfall that descends in stages. At mile 6.8, your previous turnoff, the Wolf Ridge Trail junction, is to your right. Follow the Twentymile Trail past the horse barn and back to the trailhead at mile 7.4.

Directions: From Townsend, Tennessee, drive west on US 321 and turn left onto the Foothills Parkway. Follow Foothills Parkway west to US 129. Follow US 129 south into North Carolina. Turn left on NC 28. Follow NC 28 for 2.6 miles to Twentymile Ranger Station on your left.

Park beyond the ranger station, walk up to the gated road and begin your hike on the Twentymile Trail. From the courthouse in Bryson City, North Carolina, take US 19 south for 5.4 miles to NC 28. Turn right on NC 28 and go 30 miles to Twentymile Ranger Station, which will be on your right.

Part III:
Great Overnight Loops

Cane Gap Overnight Loop

Scenery:	★★★★	Difficulty:	★★
Trail Conditions:	★★★★	Solitude:	★★★★
Children:	★★★★		

Distance: 3.8, 6.1, 2.2 miles each day
Hiking Time: 2:00, 3:00, 1:20
Outstanding Features: cemetery, swimming and fishing in summer

This is a moderate, two-night loop trip in the western lowlands that is a good break-in trip for those less experienced at toting their belongings on their backs. Travel distances are not long, offering plenty of time for fishing, exploring or just lazing around camp underneath the pines. First, you'll follow Cooper Road Trail to Cane Gap and descend to the Cane Creek campsite where you can explore the old Buchanan Cemetery. Retrace your steps, then intersect Hatcher Mountain Trail to Little Bottoms Trail and campsite, with nearby Abrams Creek offering fishing and swimming opportunities. Return to Cooper Road and the trailhead.

Start your venture on the Cooper Road Trail at the rear of the Abrams Creek campground. Follow the old road over Kingfisher Creek to the Little Bottoms Trail junction at mile 0.9. Continue on the Cooper Road Trail. Pass the Cooper Road backcountry campsite, #1, at mile 1.0, and gently rise toward Gold Mine Gap. The trail traces Kingfisher Creek for a while to arrive at Gold Mine Gap and a trail junction at mile 2.6.

Follow Cooper Road Trail down a steep hill, level off, and arrive at Cane Gap at mile 3.2. At the gap, turn left on the Cane Creek Trail (an old jeep road). Wind

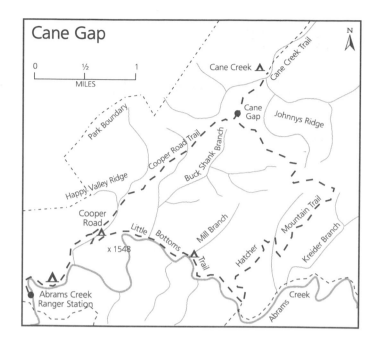

Cane Gap

0   ½   1
MILES

N

Cane Creek ▲

Cane Creek Trail

Cane Gap ●

Johnnys Ridge

Park Boundary

Cooper Road Trail

Buck Shank Branch

Happy Valley Ridge

Cooper Road ▲

Little Bottoms Trail ▲

x 1548

Mill Branch

Hatcher Mountain Trail

Kreider Branch

▲
Abrams Creek
Ranger Station ●

Creek

Abrams

your way down to cross Cane Creek just before arriving at the Cane Creek backcountry campsite, #2, at mile 3.8. This lightly used camp is your first night's destination.

Here, the intonations of Cane Creek reverberate beneath the pine and hemlock woods. Many of these trees fell in the blizzard of '93, when the weight of the wet spring snow caused the trees to collapse. A good day trip from the campsite leads to Buchanan Cemetery. A side trail takes you up a hill on your left, 1 mile beyond the campsite, on the Cane Creek Trail.

Begin day two by returning 0.6 mile to Cane Gap. Turn left, rejoining the Cooper Road Trail. Walk easily among dry woods, leveling off to rise slightly just before the Hatcher Mountain Trail junction at mile 6.1. Turn right on Hatcher Mountain in the primarily pine-oak woodlands so characteristic of the Smokies' western edge. Only when the trail dips into the hemlock and rhododendron ravine of Oak Flats Branch at mile 7.5 does it change character. Arrive at the Little Bottoms Trail junction at mile 8.9.

Turn right on the Little Bottoms Trail and wind along the side of the gorge to come to the Little Bottoms backcountry campsite, #17, at mile 9.9. This fairly popular site is your second night's destination. Little Bottoms was once an old homesite, as evidenced by the chimney, rock wall and old piles of stone in the clearing. Nearby is Abrams Creek, a fine rainbow trout fishery, providing the opportunity to drop a line or swim.

Start day three by continuing down the Little Bottoms Trail as it follows Abrams Creek to leave the gorge and ascend a side ridge. At the bottom of the side ridge lies Kingfisher Creek and the Cooper Road Trail junction at mile 11.2. Complete your loop by returning down the Cooper Road Trail, crossing Kingfisher Creek once again, to the Abrams Creek campground at mile 12.1.

Directions: From Townsend, Tennessee, drive north on US 321. Turn left off the Foothills Parkway at Chilhowee Lake onto US 129. Head south 0.5 mile to Happy Valley Road. Turn left on Happy Valley Road, following it 6 miles to Abrams Creek Road. Turn right on Abrams Creek Road and drive 1 mile to the campground, passing the ranger station. Cooper Road Trail starts at the rear of the campground. Park your car in the designated area near the ranger station.

Little River Overnight Loop

Scenery: ★★★★   Difficulty: ★★★
Trail Conditions: ★★★★   Solitude: ★★★
Children: ★★★
Distance: 5.1, 7.6, 4.8 miles each day
Hiking Time: 2:45, 4:00, 2:30
Outstanding Features: Little River, railroad relics

This overnight loop follows the Little River deep into the heart of the Smokies to a campsite in the shadow of Clingmans Dome. Then you'll climb Sugarland Mountain via Rough Creek and camp in a boulder field at the little-used Medicine Branch Bluff campsite. This trip offers creekside and ridgeline camping with a fair amount of climbing in between.

Start the camping trip on the Little River Trail, on a gentle railroad grade. The cascading Little River offers an ever-changing water show to your left. The stream crashes amid rocks, only to gather in large pools that fall again in a white, frothy mix of water and air. At mile 1.0, Huskey Branch enters the Little River in a falls above the trail that bridges the small creek. The Cucumber Gap Trail comes in from the west at mile 1.3.

Continue up the Little River, crossing it on a wide bridge just before the Huskey Gap Trail junction at mile 1.7. Stay on the east bank of the Little River, crossing several small feeder streams originating from Sugarland Mountain. The trail comes to a wide flat near the confluence of Goshen Prong and the Little River at mile 2.7. The Goshen Prong Trail bears right; stay on the Little River Trail to the Rough Creek backcountry campsite, #24, at mile 3.5.

The Little River Trail becomes somewhat rockier as it passes the Rough Creek Trail junction just beyond the Rough Creek campsite. Look for the even spacing of old railroad ties. Keep on the Little River Trail, crossing Meigs Post Prong at mile 4.7, where signs of an old railroad bridge lie about the creek bed.

Cross what's left of the small Little River at mile 5.1, where another old railroad bridge is particularly evident, and arrive at the Three Forks backcountry campsite, #30 (elevation 3,400 feet), your first night's destination. This grassy area being reclaimed by forest was once a logging camp. It is bounded on three sides by high country streams that are populated with native brook trout. These streams are closed to fishing to protect the limited habitat of the "brookie."

Start day two by backtracking 1.6 miles down the Little River Trail to the Rough Creek Trail, at mile 6.7. Turn right and begin climbing the Rough Creek Trail, which also follows an old railroad bed through second growth forest. As you climb, all sorts of remnants of the railroad days can be seen. After crossing Rough Creek twice, the trail runs north to intersect the Sugarland Mountain Trail on the narrow ridge at mile 9.5.

Turn left on the Sugarland Mountain Trail. Meander along the ridge top, maintaining a 4,500-foot elevation for the next 1.7 miles before descending around

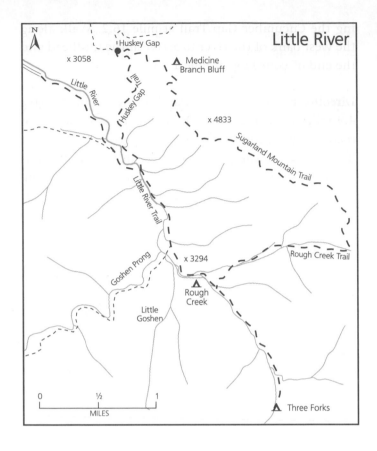

the south side of a knob on Sugarland Mountain. After working around a point in the ridge, veer into the Big Medicine Branch hollow. In a boulder field, at mile 12.7, lies the Medicine Branch Bluff backcountry campsite, #21 (elevation 3,780 feet), your second night's destination. This lightly used site is on a fair slope, but a few flat tent sites exist among the boulders. Water can be obtained from the small stream flowing at the base of the hollow.

Continue northwest on the Sugarland Mountain Trail to begin day three. You will come to Huskey Gap Trail junction at mile 13.7 of the loop. Turn left on the Huskey Gap Trail, an old pre-park crossroads, descending beyond the drainages of Big Medicine Branch and Phoebe Branch to enter a wide, flat area in the vicinity of the Little River. Arrive at the Little River Trail junction just after crossing Sugar Orchard Branch, at mile 15.8.

Head down the Little River Trail, once again passing the Cucumber Gap Trail at mile 16.2. Walk along the west bank of the river to arrive at the trailhead and the end of your loop at mile 17.5.

Directions: From the Sugarland Visitor Center, drive 4.9 miles to turn left into Elkmont. Follow the paved road 1.3 miles to the Elkmont campground. Turn left just before the campground check-in station and follow the somewhat rough road 0.7 mile to the parking area at the end of Little River Road. The Little River Trail starts at the end of the gated road.

Maddron Bald Overnight Loop

Scenery:	★★★★★	Difficulty:	★★★
Trail Conditions:	★★★★	Solitude:	★★★★
Children:	★★		

Distance: 4.8, 6.2, 6.8 miles each day
Hiking Time: 2:45, 3:45, 3:55
Outstanding Features: Henwallow Falls, old growth forest, Maddron Bald views

This two-night trip is one of if not the best backpacking loops in the entire park! First, hike along the lower reaches of Gabes Mountain, passing Henwallow Falls, and enter virgin woodland to camp at Sugar Cove. Then head up the Maddron Bald Trail to Albright Grove, which contains some of the park's largest trees. Camp along a resonant high country creek near Maddron Bald, which sports awe-inspiring views both above and below. On the return trip down the rugged Snake Den Trail, a few more vistas open up on some smaller heath balds. This excursion exemplifies the Smoky Mountains at their finest.

Your trip starts on the Gabes Mountain Trail. You'll cross several branches of Crying Creek on footlogs before arriving at an old road turnaround at mile 1.1. While climbing the side of Gabes Mountain, pass amid crumbling homesites scattered in the second growth woods along the old road. A newly graded side trail leads to the foot of Henwallow Falls at mile 2.1.

After the falls, continue right on the Gabes Mountain Trail and enter an old growth forest. Large, slick-surfaced beech trees and huge hemlocks stand out among the giants. The trail crosses small brooks that carve through the mountainside and feed the fern and rhododendron understory.

Ford Greenbrier Creek at mile 4.8 and reach the Sugar Cove backcountry campsite, #34 (elevation 3,240 feet). This is your first night's destination. The campsite gets a fair amount of use but is in good shape, with camping areas lining the creek.

The next day, continue westward on the Gabes Mountain Trail. Slowly snake your way along Cole Creek; the trail crosses Cole Creek and its tributaries so many times that you'll think Cole Creek is the trail. Don't forget to look up at all the big trees above as you rock hop over the watercourses. At mile 6.6, the trail arrives at the Maddron Bald Trail junction.

Turn left up the Maddron Bald Trail past the boulder in the middle of the road. Come to an old road turn-around at mile 7.7 of your loop hike. The trail becomes a rocky footpath, crossing Indian Camp Creek on a footlog at mile 8.2. The view up the creek is quite picturesque. Rounding the point of a small ridge, you'll come to the Albright Grove Nature Trail at mile 8.3.

Turn right on the nature trail and see some reasons for the establishment of this national park. Old growth Carolina silverbells, hemlocks, beech and tulip trees have been spared the logger's axe and now enjoy national park protection along this 0.7-mile trail winding among

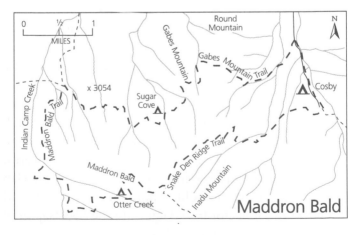

the giants that lie between Indian Camp and Dunn creeks. Return to the Maddron Bald Trail at mile 9.0.

The Maddron Bald Trail ascends along and through Indian Camp and Copperhead creeks, leaving the cove to round the point of a ridge at mile 10.5. A small trail to your left emerges at a rocky overlook among crowded brush. From the overlook you can see the town of Cosby below. To your left is Snag Mountain. Up and to your right is Maddron Bald.

Keep ascending on the Maddron Bald Trail to reach the Otter Creek backcountry campsite, #29 (elevation 4,560 feet), at mile 11.0. This is your second night's destination. In this series of small level areas, there once sat a small Civilian Conservation Corps camp. A pulley-operated food hanging device, with directions, has been erected for your convenience. The wind rushes through the Otter Creek hollow throughout the year. Maddron Bald, a mere half-mile away, makes a good day hike from the camp.

Day three starts with the climb away from Otter Creek and up to Maddron Bald at mile 11.5. This heath bald has low, dense bush cover rather than grass cover, with the occasional rock outcrop to take in the out-standing views. The state line ridge stands above to your south; the lower Smokies and beyond expand to your north. The near and the far come with this view.

Beyond the bald, reenter the forest and intersect the Snake Den Ridge Trail at mile 12.5. This is the high point of the trip (elevation 5,800 feet), with the telltale high country spruce and fir trees about. Turn left on the Snake Den Ridge Trail and start working your way down on a set of switchbacks. Occasionally, on the dry ridge tops, you'll be able to see over the heath bald-like cover to view the crest of the Smokies to your right.

At mile 15.2, the trail crosses Inadu Creek. It then works its way northeast down a cove to cross Rock Creek on a footlog at mile 16.2. Soon the trail comes into an old road turnaround and enters a previously settled area. A trail linking Snake Den Ridge Trail to the Low Gap Trail enters from the right at mile 16.8. Turn right and follow the connector trail 0.6 mile to the Low Gap Trail junction. Turn left and follow the Low Gap Trail 0.4 mile down to the hiker parking area at mile 17.8, completing the loop.

Directions: From Gatlinburg, take US 321 east until it comes to a "T" intersection with TN 32. Turn right on TN 32 and follow it a little over 1 mile, turning right into the signed Cosby section of the park. At 2.1 miles on Cosby Road, arrive at the hiker parking area on the left, near the campground registration hut. Backtrack down Cosby Road 0.1 mile to the picnic area. The Gabes Mountain Trail starts across the road from the picnic area.

Mount Sterling Overnight Loop

Scenery:	★★★★★	Difficulty:	★★★
Trail Conditions:	★★★★	Solitude:	★★★★
Children:	★★★		

Distance: 5.1, 6.0, 6.2 miles each day
Hiking Time: 3:00, 4:00, 3:45
Outstanding Features: Big Creek, Walnut Bottoms, views from Mount Sterling

Start this trip at Big Creek Ranger Station (an out-of-the way yet easily accessible departure point) for a trip along Big Creek and into the high country. Follow an old road on a gentle grade to Walnut Bottoms. Camp where several streams come together, providing ample fishing waters for those so inclined. Then climb the rigorous Swallow Fork Trail to the high country on Mount Sterling Ridge. Some pleasant ridge walking leads to Mount Sterling and your second night's destination at the highest unsheltered backcountry campsite in the park. Pass through old growth forest on your descent along the Baxter Creek Trail back to Big Creek where the loop ends.

Proceed up the Big Creek Trail past the gate and follow what was once an Indian path, then a logging railroad, and finally an auto road, until it returned to being a horse and footpath. Parallel Big Creek, an exceptionally attractive mountain stream, to pass the Rock

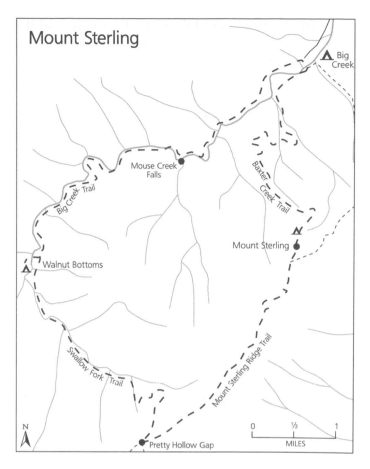

Mount Sterling

Big Creek
Mouse Creek Falls
Big Creek Trail
Baxter Creek Trail
Mount Sterling
Walnut Bottoms
Swallow Fork Trail
Mount Sterling Ridge Trail

N

0   ½   1
MILES

Pretty Hollow Gap

House on the right at mile 1.0. Once home for logging families until they could obtain better quarters, the Rock House provides shelter from the summer thunderstorms so prevalent in the Smokies.

Mouse Creek Falls spills into Big Creek on your left at mile 2.1. A wide Civilian Conservation Corps-built bridge spans Big Creek at mile 2.3. One of the Smokies' best-named and most famous springs appears on the left at mile 2.8. Brakeshoe Spring, christened for a railroad brake placed there by an engineer with a fondness for Smoky Mountain water, emerges on the left. The brake shoe is gone; only the name remains.

Continue following Big Creek as it horseshoes up the valley and ford Flint Rock Cove Branch at mile 4.3. At mile 5.0, come to the Swallow Fork Trail junction. Stay on the Big Creek Trail and cross the bridge over Big Creek to enter the Lower Walnut Bottoms backcountry campsite, #37 (elevation 3,000 feet), at mile 5.1, your first night's destination. This campsite is popular among both hikers and bears, so food storage boxes and hanging poles are provided to help keep the bears wild and hikers stocked with the provisions they brought. Do not leave food lying about.

Begin day two by crossing the bridge back over Big Creek and turning right on the Swallow Fork Trail at mile 5.2 of your loop hike. The ascent is a fairly gentle-graded trail until McGinty Creek, where it steepens considerably. At mile 6.0, the Swallow Fork Trail crosses Swallow Fork on a footlog. Cross McGinty Creek at mile 6.3, and after passing a mountain flat, begin the pull to Pretty Hollow Gap. Leave the Swallow Fork hollow, making a severe right turn at mile 8.5 to switchback up to Pretty Hollow Gap and the spruce-fir high country nearly a mile in elevation, at mile 9.2.

Turn left on the Mount Sterling Ridge Trail, ascending out of the gap to a small knob flanked by fragrant evergreen trees. Briefly descend, then make the push for Mount Sterling. When you come to the Mount Sterling Trail junction at mile 10.6, pass straight through. The trail changes names at this point, from the Mount Sterling Ridge Trail to the Mount Sterling Trail. Pass through grassy and forested areas and beyond a horse-hitch rack on your right, just before topping out on Mount Sterling at mile 11.1.

A fire tower adorns the top of Mount Sterling, offering a 360-degree view. Be very careful on this or any other fire tower. Below the tower is the Mount Sterling backcountry campsite, #38 (elevation 5,800 feet). This is your second night's destination. Water can be obtained on a side path to your left as you go a half-mile down the Baxter Creek Trail, which starts near the fire tower. Various designated campsites are sheltered among the evergreens below the tower. Note: The weather can be severe on Mount Sterling any time of the year.

Day three begins with the descent of the Baxter Creek Trail. Pass the spring-side trail at mile 11.6 of your loop hike, as you work your way down the old growth Canadian-type forest. More switchbacks lead to and beyond the point of Mount Sterling Ridge at mile 13.3. The downgrade remains remarkably consistent until you enter the Baxter Creek valley, and first cross a branch of Baxter Creek at mile 15.6, then cross Baxter Creek itself at mile 16.0. Continue along the east bank of Baxter Creek, crossing Big Creek on a footbridge before arriving at the Big Creek picnic area at mile 17.3, completing your loop.

Directions: From I-40, take the Waterville exit, #451. Cross the Pigeon River, then turn left to follow it upstream for 2.3 miles until you come to an intersection. Proceed forward through the intersection and soon afterward enter the park. Pass the Big Creek Ranger Station and come to the Big Creek picnic area at mile 3.4. Park here and backtrack a short distance to the Big Creek trailhead.

Spruce Mountain Overnight Loop

Scenery: ★★★★★   Difficulty: ★★★
Trail Conditions: ★★★   Solitude: ★★★★
Children: ★★
Distance Per Day: 4.6, 9.7, 7.4 miles
Hiking Time Per Day: 2:45, 5:30, 4:30
Outstanding Features: Big Poplars, history, views,
                                        Palmer Creek

The Spruce Mountain overnight loop is an outstanding two-night trip that covers a wide variety of terrain and trail conditions while offering a good opportunity for solitude. It must be noted, however, that a portion of the loop requires a short connection down a lightly used gravel road, which is closed to traffic in the winter. You'll leave the grassy Cataloochee Valley and ascend to the spruce-fir high country. Hikers with sharp eyes can spot the valley below to mark their progress.

The trip begins at the Big Fork Ridge trailhead with an immediate crossing over Rough Fork on a footbridge. Shortly, the trail passes an old pioneer farm site, as evidenced by the fields now being reclaimed by the forest. Begin ascending the ridge, winding upwards to

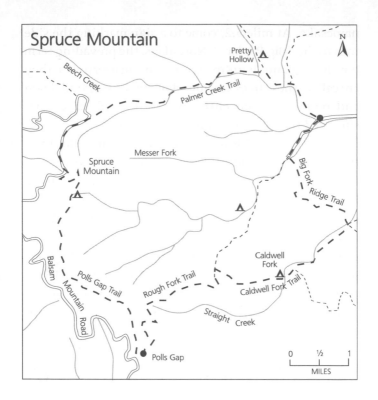

Spruce Mountain

reach a gap in Big Fork Ridge at mile 1.7. Pass through the gap and enter the watershed of Caldwell Fork. Soon you'll hear its noisy waters. A footbridge makes for a dry crossing of Caldwell Fork. Climb briefly away from the creek to intersect the Caldwell Fork Trail at mile 3.1.

Turn right and follow the trail up along Caldwell Fork. Heavy horse traffic often renders this trail muddy. At mile 3.2, pass the McKee Branch Trail junction. A small side trail leads uphill to a gravesite at mile 3.4. Two Union soldiers of ill repute are buried there. Continuing on, intersect the Hemphill Bald Trail at mile 4.5. Cross Double Gap Branch and arrive at the Caldwell Fork backcountry campsite, #41, at mile 4.6. This is your first night's destination.

The site offers many camping areas, either under shady hemlocks or out in the open at the former homesite. Explore the area, looking for signs of the early pioneers. Leave all artifacts in their place, as they comprise a living archaeological exhibit.

After spending your first night out, proceed up the Caldwell Fork Trail as it begins to climb away from its namesake. At mile 5.2, come to a sign marking the side trail to the "Big Poplars." Nowadays, the prevailing term for these giants is tulip tree but no matter what they are called, these trees are huge. Follow the side trail down and ponder the immensity of centuries-old trees that survived the logging era in the Smokies.

Back on the Caldwell Fork Trail, climb away from the former farmland, passing through old growth forest to a prominent gap and beyond, to intersect the Rough Fork Trail at mile 6.3. Veer left and continue ascending, looking for views of the Cataloochee Valley below. At mile 7.8, come to an old railroad grade that makes for wide and easy walking. Fragrant red spruce trees start to appear, a sign of the high country. Their sharp, squared-off needles distinguish them from fir and hemlocks. Polls Gap and its parking area appear at mile 9.8.

Turn right and follow the rutted and rocky Polls Gap Trail up the ridge to top out on Cataloochee Balsam (elevation 5,970 feet) at mile 11.4. Leave the mountain top, clambering over the many blown-down trees. After passing through Horse Creek Gap, the trail climbs again to Chiltoes Mountain at mile 13.0.

Turn right down the short side trail that is marked by a sign, at mile 14.2, to reach the Spruce Mountain backcountry campsite, #42. This is a small, lightly used camp, one of the higher backcountry sites in the park, lying over a mile in elevation. A dim trail at the lower edge of the camp leads to a reliable spring.

After a night in the cool high country, return to the Polls Gap Trail and turn right. Go 0.1 mile to intersect the Spruce Mountain Trail. (To the right, 1.0 mile distant, is the top of Spruce Mountain and the former site of a fire tower, which makes a nice day trip from campsite #42.) Follow the Spruce Mountain Trail down to the left 1.0 mile to Balsam Mountain Road at mile 15.3 of your loop.

Turn right on the gravel road and follow it 1.8 miles to the Palmer Creek Trail on the right. The trail quickly descends through a long rhododendron tunnel that emerges into a more open forest. At mile 18.7, cross

Beech Creek. Then, as the Palmer Creek valley narrows, cross Lost Bottom Creek on a footlog at mile 19.3. Continuing to descend, the Palmer Creek Trail intersects the Pretty Hollow Trail after crossing Pretty Hollow Creek on another footlog at mile 20.4. Turn right, following Pretty Hollow Creek on a wide jeep trail through some clearings, passing the Little Cataloochee Trail junction at mile 20.9. A mere 0.8 mile farther is the loop's end at Cataloochee Road. Follow the road up the valley a short ways and return to your vehicle.

Directions: Leave I-40 at exit 20 to NC 276. In a short distance reach Cove Creek Road, which you follow nearly 6 miles to enter the park. Travel 2 miles beyond the park boundary, then turn left onto Cataloochee Road. Follow it to the end. The Big Fork Ridge Trail is on the left just before you reach the parking area.

Hughes Ridge Overnight Loop

Scenery: ★★★★   Difficulty: ★★★
Trail Conditions: ★★★   Solitude: ★★★★
Children: ★
Distance: 3.3, 4.8, 10.5 miles each day
Hiking Time: 2:00, 2:45, 6:00
Outstanding Features: old growth trees, remote Raven
Fork gorge

Raven Fork Gorge offers some of the most rugged terrain in the Smokies. First, leave Smokemont on the Bradley Fork Trail, to turn right up the Chasteen Creek Trail, and camp at the luxuriant head of Chasteen Creek Cove. Then make the steep climb to Hughes Ridge, hiking north a short distance along the ridge to intersect the Enloe Creek Trail. Descend along Enloe Creek to camp on Raven Fork, where cabin-sized boulders are strewn about the watercourse, hemmed in by jungle-like growth. Return to Hughes Ridge and amble along the wooded knobs through Cherokee Reservation territory and back into the park to complete your loop.

Start the circuit by leaving the Smokemont campground on the Bradley Fork Trail. Stay on the east side

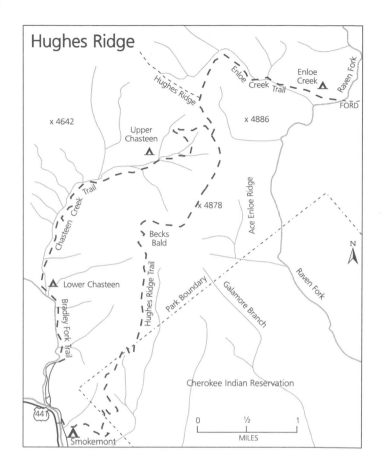

Hughes Ridge

x 4642

Upper Chasteen ⛺

Hughes Ridge

Enloe Creek Trail

Enloe Creek ⛺

Raven Fork

FORD

x 4886

x 4878

Ace Enloe Ridge

Chasteen Creek Trail

Becks Bald

Lower Chasteen ⛺

Bradley Fork Trail

Hughes Ridge Trail

Park Boundary

Galamore Branch

Raven Fork

N

Cherokee Indian Reservation

441

Smokemont ⛺

0   ½   1

MILES

of Bradley Fork and cross Chasteen Creek on a wide bridge at mile 1.0. Turn right just beyond this crossing at the Chasteen Creek Trail junction. The Chasteen Creek backcountry campsite, #50, is at the beginning of the Chasteen Creek Trail. Pass the campsite, cross Chasteen Creek on a bridge and begin the less strenuous portion of the Chasteen Creek Trail that lies between Bradley Fork and the first night's destination 2.3 miles distant.

Follow an old roadbed, which is sometimes muddy, that lines the east bank of strikingly pretty Chasteen Creek. At mile 1.9, cross a brook flowing down from Becks Bald, high on Hughes Ridge. Once past a horse hitching post, the trail is less used. At mile 3.3, come to the Upper Chasteen backcountry campsite, #48 (elevation 3,320 feet). This is your first night's destination, in the head of a lush cove where small feeder streams converge from the surrounding heights to form Chasteen Creek.

Day two starts by leaving the now crude jeep road in a turnaround just below the 3,700-foot elevation, at mile 3.9. The trail narrows and begins to switchback its way up the western side of Hughes Ridge. Climb steeply to arrive in a saddle of Hughes Ridge and a trail junction at mile 5.1 of your loop hike.

Turn left on Hughes Ridge Trail. Travel northward, leaving the saddle to come to the Enloe Creek Trail junction at mile 5.6. Turn right on the Enloe Creek Trail and begin switchbacking down through essentially unlogged forest; into the steep-sided, heavily wooded Enloe Creek gorge. Follow the right bank of Enloe Creek as it makes a southeasterly turn toward Raven Fork.

Just before crossing Enloe Creek on a footbridge at mile 7.2, you'll slog your way through the most consistently muddy section of trail in the entire park. Beyond the footbridge, the trail stays on the ridgeside as the creek crashes its way down to merge with Raven Fork. Come to Raven Fork and the Enloe Creek backcountry campsite, #47 (elevation 3,620 feet), at mile 8.2. This is your second night's destination.

A large steel bridge spans Raven Fork at this small campsite, the only open area for miles along the Raven Fork watershed. Stand on the bridge and look out on Raven Fork. Up and down the creek huge boulders have come to rest amid the flowing waters. If you choose to fish or explore this rough area, exercise extreme caution, as many people have been hurt here and rescue is very difficult and dangerous.

Start day three by retracing your steps back to Hughes Ridge, spanning Enloe Creek once again, at mile 9.2 of your loop hike. Parallel Enloe Creek, then switchback up to Hughes Ridge to arrive at a trail junction at mile 10.8. Turn left on Hughes Ridge Trail, passing the Chasteen Creek Trail junction at mile 11.3. Continue a southerly course along the Hughes Ridge. Here the trail undulates between small knobs and sags.

Skirt the right flank of the now wooded Becks Bald at mile 13.7, leaving the ridge top. Pass by the only water source you'll encounter on the ridge, a small rill in a hollow on the west side of Becks Bald, at mile 14.2. Begin a steady descent to enter reservation territory, only to switchback into the park and out again.

The next section can be confusing, as various horse trails intersect the Hughes Ridge Trail. Shortly after you enter the park again (noted by a rectangular, green-and-white park service sign), a horse trail enters from the right at mile 17.7. Stay left. Bear right at the next horse trail junction, 0.4 mile beyond the first. Cross a small brook and veer right at the next intersection to arrive at the road below the Smokemont campground at mile 18.6, to complete your loop. Return to your car by following the road past the bridge with the Oconaluftee River flowing downstream to your left, passing the campground registration hut and coming to the parking area at the rear of the Smokemont campground.

Directions: From the Oconaluftee Visitor Center, drive 3.2 miles north on Newfound Gap Road. Turn right into the Smokemont campground on a bridge over the Oconaluftee River. Veer left and pass the campground check-in station. The Bradley Fork Trail starts at the gated jeep road at the right rear of the campground.

Newton Bald Overnight Loop

Scenery:	★★★★	Difficulty:	★★★
Trail Conditions:	★★★★	Solitude:	★★★
Children:	★★		

Distance: 6.3, 7.0, 9.8 miles each day
Hiking Time: 4:00, 4:45, 5:30
Outstanding Features: history, Deep Creek, ridge walking

On this trip, you'll head up the famed fishing waters of Deep Creek, the origin of many a Smoky Mountain hunting and fishing tale, to camp at a streamside site on a carpet of pine needles beneath a grove of white pines. Then leave the Deep Creek watershed, via the steep Martins Gap Trail, to intersect Sunkota Ridge Trail for some nice ridge walking to a little-used backcountry camp 5,000 feet high on Thomas Ridge. Finally, head south on the ridge, running Thomas Divide Trail back to Deep Creek to complete the loop.

Begin the hike on the Deep Creek Trail, which starts out as a gravel road, passing the Indian Creek Trail junction at mile 0.7. Cross Indian Creek on a bridge and continue up Deep Creek Trail to a road turnaround at mile 2.2, crossing three bridges and passing the Loop Trail junction along the way. Leave the road to follow a graded trail that traverses Bumgardner Branch, and arrive at the Bumgardner Branch backcountry campsite, #60, at mile 2.9. Stay on the east bank of Deep Creek, which rises far above the creek. An historic wagon road once forded the creek here.

Drop down to the McCracken Branch backcountry campsite, #59, at mile 4.2. Repeat the pattern of rise and fall to enter Nicks Nest Branch backcountry campsite, #58, at mile 5.7. Trace the right bank of Deep Creek, coming to the historic Bryson Place and a trail junction at mile 6.0. Once the site of a backwoods cabin and a hunting lodge, this was a favorite haunt of famed outdoor writer and national park proponent Horace Kephart. Of course, fishing continues to be a recreational pastime of many Smokies visitors.

Leave Bryson Place on the Deep Creek Trail and come to the Burnt Spruce backcountry campsite, #56 (elevation 2,405 feet), at mile 6.3. Spend your first night here, under the big white pines, with Deep Creek rushing nearby. This campsite rests nestled between two others that receive heavier usage, Bryson Place and Pole Road; thus it remains a fine creekside camp.

Day two begins by returning to Bryson Place, 0.3 mile back down the Deep Creek Trail. Turn left up the Martins Gap Trail, climbing steeply 1.5 miles to Martins Gap at mile 8.1 of your loop hike. Turn left on the infrequently trodden Sunkota Ridge Trail, gently ascending out of Martins Gap around the east side of a knob. Continue ascending, passing a spring at mile 9.5. It seems that the trail will top out, yet it keeps gaining elevation in moderate spurts between level areas to intersect the Thomas Divide Trail at mile 12.9 (elevation 4,780 feet).

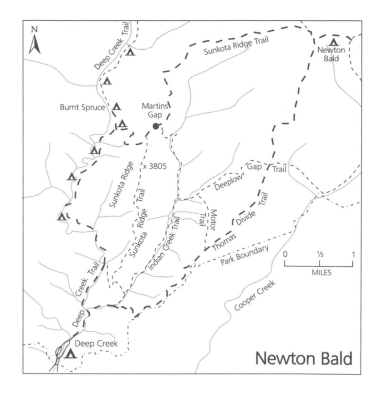

Newton Bald

Turn right on the Thomas Divide Trail and walk 0.4 mile to arrive at the Newton Bald Trail junction. Turn left on the Newton Bald Trail, following it 0.1 mile and coming to the Newton Bald backcountry campsite, #52, your second night's destination. This 5,000-foot-high campsite, located in a saddle on Thomas Divide near what was once an open meadow, is a favorable place to escape the summer heat and crowds. In the winter, Newton Bald is susceptible to strong winds. Chestnut trees still grow on this former bald, but they don't get very big; after a few year's growth, they succumb to the same chestnut blight that wiped out the Smokies' most prolific food-bearing tree in the 1920s.

Start day three by backtracking 0.1 mile to the Thomas Divide Trail. Turn left and begin a southwesterly course toward Deep Creek Ranger Station. Walk among wooded knolls around the 5,000-foot elevation for nearly 2 miles, then begin a prolonged descent, passing the Deeplow Gap Trail at mile 16.5 of your loop hike. Climb out of Deeplow Gap and begin an undulating course on the ridge.

At mile 18.9, intersect what was once the Indian Creek Motor Nature Trail, begun in the 1960s but halted due to public outcry. The roadbed, running parallel to the park boundary, makes for easy walking as you continually lose elevation. Still on the Thomas Divide Trail, come to a trail junction at mile 21.0. Turn right on the Stone Pile Gap Trail and continue your descent, zigzagging over the small creek that often muddies the trail.

Intersect the Indian Creek Trail at mile 22.0 and turn left. Pass by Indian Creek Falls on your right, then come to another trail junction at mile 22.4. Turn left on the Deep Creek Trail and follow it 0.7 mile to complete your 23.1-mile loop.

Directions: From the Oconaluftee Visitor Center, take US 441 south to Cherokee, North Carolina. Turn right on US 19 and drive 10 miles to Bryson City, North Carolina. Turn right at the Swain County Courthouse onto Everett Street and carefully follow the signs through town to the Deep Creek campground. The Deep Creek Trail is at the back of the campground.

Springhouse Branch Overnight Loop

Scenery:	★★★★	Difficulty:	★★
Trail Conditions:	★★★★	Solitude:	★★★
Children:	★★★		

Distance: 5.4, 10.4, 7.2 miles each day
Hiking Time: 3:00, 5:30, 4:00
Outstanding Features: history, creekside environment, virgin forest

If you enjoy the magic of an ever-moving, ever-changing Smoky Mountain stream, this trip is for you. Hike north into the Noland Creek watershed, passing several old homesites, to camp at Jerry Flats. Then take the Springhouse Branch Trail into virgin forest over Forney Ridge and into the Forney Creek watershed, passing an old Civilian Conservation Corps camp. Continue up Forney Creek to camp where Jonas Creek flows into

Forney Creek. Return along Forney Creek to the Whiteoak Branch Trail, then exit at the end of the "Road to Nowhere" through an abandoned tunnel.

Start your trip at the lower end of the Noland Creek parking area. Follow this short trail down to the Noland Creek Trail. Turn right on the Noland Creek Trail, passing under the Noland Creek bridge on Lakeview Drive, then over a bridge spanning Noland Creek at mile 0.3. Continue up the old road, passing the side trail to the Bear Pen Branch backcountry campsite, #65, at mile 1.3 on the Noland Creek Trail.

Cross cascading Noland Creek on a second bridge in an area of old homesites at mile 1.9. Look around for stone foundations and chimneys. Span Noland Creek on a wide bridge at mile 2.7 and 4.0. You are now in the Solola Valley, which housed enough people to warrant its own school. At mile 4.2 lies the Mill Creek backcountry campsite, #64, which is primarily used by horse campers.

To the left is the Springhouse Branch Trail. Veer right and stay on the Noland Creek Trail, immediately crossing Noland Creek on a footlog. After the crossing you'll spot an abandoned ranger station, hidden among the trees. Continue the moderate ascension up the right bank of Noland Creek to cross the creek once more on a footlog at mile 5.0. After 0.4 mile, come upon the Jerry Flats backcountry campsite, #63 (elevation 2,920 feet). This is your first night's destination. The campsite is flat and fairly open, probably an old homesite.

After a night in Jerry Flats, start day two by returning down Noland Creek Trail 1.2 miles, to intersect the Springhouse Branch Trail at mile 6.6 of your loop hike. Turn right up the Springhouse Branch Trail, immediately crossing Mill Creek twice in succession among the rhododendron. At mile 7.1, rock piles, washtubs and an old chimney are evidence of pre-park settlement in this interesting area. Turn westward after crossing Mill Creek on a footlog, still in previously settled country.

Ascend along Springhouse Branch and enter virgin woods, crossing small feeder streams in the mountain cove before winding around the point of a ridge at mile

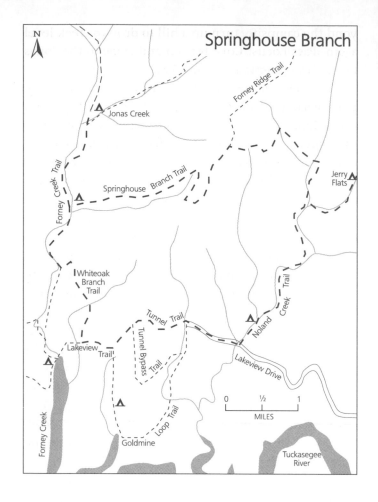

8.4. Work up the side of Forney Ridge, and come to Board Camp Gap and a trail junction at mile 9.4. An old shack of rough-hewn boards once stood here, giving the gap its name.

Climb southward out of the gap, still on the Springhouse Branch Trail, turning away from Rough Hew Ridge. After a switchback, turn north and cross Bee Gum Branch at mile 11.1. Begin descending on the north side of Bee Gum Branch hollow. Two prominent switchbacks signal your imminent arrival at Forney Creek. After crossing Bee Gum Branch, pass through the CCC backcountry campsite, #71, to intersect the Forney Creek Trail at mile 14.8. Turn right on the Forney Creek Trail and pass amid Civilian Conservation Corps relics such as barrels, a chimney, even an old bathtub. Beyond the campsite, turn up a hill to drop to creek level again. Pass Locust Cove Branch and come to the Jonas Creek Trail junction at mile 15.8.

Turn left on the Jonas Creek Trail and immediately cross Forney Creek on a long footlog. Just beyond a rhododendron thicket is the Jonas Creek backcountry campsite, #70 (elevation 2,400 feet). This is your second night's destination. Jonas and Forney creeks, on either side of the large, level campsite backed up against a steep hill, will sing you to sleep when night falls.

Start day three by crossing Forney Creek back to the Forney Creek Trail. Turn right on the Forney Creek Trail and return to the CCC backcountry campsite, at mile 16.8 of your loop hike. Continue along the creek to climb away up the side of a hill, avoiding the tough fords of the old Forney Creek Trail. Drop to the crashing stream, only to climb once again. Intersect the Whiteoak Branch Trail at mile 18.0. Turn left up the Whiteoak Branch Trail, crossing Whiteoak Branch to top out in a gap. As you begin descending, signs of human presence appear along Gray Wolf Creek. Turn left away from an old road that parallels Gray Wolf Creek and intersect the Lakeshore Trail in an old homesite clearing at mile 20.0.

Turn left on the Lakeshore Trail and begin ascending along a rill over a gap leading to the Goldmine Loop Trail junction at mile 21.5. Shortly, intersect the Tunnel Bypass Trail and continue another 0.5 mile to the tunnel that was the final project of the "Road to Nowhere." Once in the tunnel, let your eyes adjust to the dimness, and you'll see the light at the tunnel's end. When outside again, enter the parking area at the end of Lakeview Drive, the official name of the "Road to Nowhere." A less than ideal 0.7 mile of road walking leads to the Noland Creek parking area, the loop's end.

Directions: From the Oconaluftee Visitor Center, head south on Newfound Gap Road for 3.2 miles to US 19 in Cherokee, North Carolina. Turn right on US 19 and follow it 10 miles to Bryson City, North Carolina. Once in Bryson City, turn right at the courthouse and continue straight on Everett Street, which becomes Lakeview Drive. The Noland Creek parking area is on the left, 5 miles beyond the park border.

Fontana Lake Overnight Loop

Scenery: ★★★★★   Difficulty: ★★
Trail Conditions: ★★★★   Solitude: ★★
Children: ★★★★
Distance: 4.7, 6.8, 6.2 miles each day
Hiking Time: 2:45, 4:00, 3:45
Outstanding Features: lakeside camping, history,
                      good initiation backpack

If you like a combination of mountains and lakes, this moderate hike is for you and any younger or inexperienced backpackers you may wish to bring along. Start your trip with a pleasurable boat ride from Fontana Marina to Hazel Creek. Hike up a modest grade on the Lakeshore Trail, through a valley steeped in settler and logging history, to camp at Sugar Fork, one of the Smokies' best campsites. Then cross over Jenkins Trail Ridge to the Eagle Creek watershed. Camping right where Eagle Creek spills into Fontana Lake, you'll enjoy both a tumbling stream and a mountain-rimmed lake. On your return, pass more history on the Lakeshore Trail, intersect the Appalachian Trail and walk over Fontana Dam (the highest in the East) to the Fontana Marina.

Before you leave, contact Fontana Marina at (704) 498-2211, extension 277, to arrange for a one-way shuttle; you'll hike back to the marina. Your trip begins at the mouth of Hazel Creek on the Lakeshore Trail. Pass the Proctor Creek backcountry campsite, #86, at mile 0.5. Soon, cross Hazel Creek on a wide bridge; the house across the creek is park owned and used. Hike along the jeep road and watch for the many signs of the homestead and logging days. On your left at mile 1.2 is the old Proctor cemetery.

As you hike, scenic Hazel Creek comes into view. Cross two wide bridges before arriving at the Sawdust Pile backcountry campsite, #85, on your right at mile

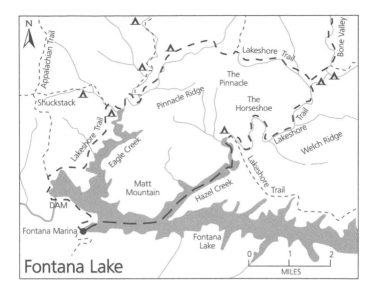

Fontana Lake

3.3. Span two more bridges before coming to a trail junction at mile 4.5. To your right, just across the bridge over Sugar Fork, is the Sugar Fork backcountry camp site, #84 (elevation 2,160 feet). This is your first night's destination.

Nestled between Sugar Fork and Hazel Creek, this level campsite beneath the pines makes an ideal base camp for the angler or amateur archaeologist. A thick metal wire is strung between two trees at the camp to aid in hanging your food away from bears and raccoons, both of which have presented problems in the past.

Start day two by crossing the wooden bridge over Sugar Fork and rejoining the Lakeshore Trail as it heads west over Jenkins Trail Ridge. Follow an old road high above Sugar Fork, passing a side trail on your left to the Higdon Cemetery, at mile 5.0 of your loop hike. As you climb, notice how well the forest has recovered from being completely logged in the first quarter of the twentieth century. At mile 6.2, on the right up Little Fork, is the site of a former copper mine and homestead. More climbing leads to Pickens Gap on Jenkins Trail Ridge, and a trail junction, at mile 6.9.

Stay on the Lakeshore Trail and begin descending fairly steeply on switchbacks. At mile 7.5, cross Pinnacle Creek, for the first of 16 times, many of them possibly wet crossings. Continue descending along the north bank of Pinnacle Creek to arrive at the small Pinnacle Creek backcountry campsite, #88, at mile 9.1. Just beyond the campsite, the Lakeshore Trail and Pinnacle Creek merge into one, the Lakeshore Trail crossing and re-crossing Pinnacle Creek on the journey to Eagle Creek.

Emerge from the junglesque rhododendron thickets of Pinnacle Creek to reach Eagle Creek at mile 10.5. Thankfully, a very long footlog spans Eagle Creek and spares you one more ford. Cross Eagle Creek and immediately come to the Eagle Creek Trail junction. Turn left and stay on the Lakeshore Trail, which now parallels Eagle Creek.

Cross Eagle Creek on a another footlog, then on a new metal frame bridge at mile 10.8. Veer right and the lake comes into view on your left. Pass over Lost Cove Creek on a footlog to arrive at the Lost Cove backcountry campsite, #90 (elevation 1,760 feet), at mile 11.3. This is your second night's destination. The popular campsite extends out beyond the trees and offers fishing and swimming in both Fontana Lake and nearby mountain streams.

Start day three by finding the Lost Cove Trail. As you look out on the lake from the campsite, the Lost Cove Trail will be uphill and to your right. Hike up the Lost Cove Trail, and in 0.4 mile, you'll find a junction on your left. Take the Lakeshore Trail, which has many old roads and trails leading off it; make sure you stay on the right trail. Fontana Lake will be on your left the whole way.

The trail will follow a pattern: up and around a point of a ridge and down into a creek-filled hollow, up the side of a ridge and over the point and down into a hollow again. At mile 14.6 of your loop hike, intersect an old road that still has some junk cars from the 1930s nearby. Homesites and other evidence of settlers are all about this section of trail. Leave the road at mile 16.4, to climb to another old road that leads out to Fontana Dam Road at mile 17.1.

Reach the north side of Fontana Dam at mile 17.7, intersecting the Appalachian Trail along the way. Follow the A.T. to the left away from Fontana Dam Road and pass a trail shelter, known as the "Fontana Hilton" because it is so nice. After a brief time in the woods, the A.T. crosses a road leading to the marina. The marina is a short distance downhill to your left. Turn left on the road and complete your loop.

Directions: From Townsend, Tennessee, take US 321 north to the Foothills Parkway. Follow Foothills Parkway west to US 129. Turn south on US 129 into North Carolina. Turn left on NC 28, passing Fontana Village. Go 1.5 miles past Fontana Village entrance and turn left at the sign to Fontana Dam. Then turn right at the sign to Fontana Village Marina, a short distance away. From Bryson City, North Carolina, take US 19 south to NC 28. Follow NC 28 for nearly 25 miles to turn right at the sign to Fontana Dam, then right to Fontana Village Marina.

Gregory Bald Overnight Loop

Scenery: ★★★★★   Difficulty: ★★★
Trail Conditions: ★★★★   Solitude: ★★★★
Children: ★★
Distance: 4.1, 4.6, 7.0 miles each day
Hiking Time: 2:30, 3:00, 4:00
Outstanding Features: good campsites, high country
meadows

This hike combines the best that the high and low country have to offer. First, you'll travel up the Twentymile Trail past Twentymile Cascades to the Upper Flats streamside camp. Then an arduous climb tops out on Long Hungry Ridge and leads to the Gregory Bald Trail, arriving at the southern Appalachians most famous bald, with its staggering views and flower displays. Camp at Sheep Pen Gap, a high country grassy glade between Gregory Bald and Parson Bald. Leave the grassy balds and complete your loop via the steep Wolf Ridge Trail.

Start your hike on the Twentymile Trail, following it to the Wolf Ridge Trail junction at mile 0.6. Turn right, passing the side trail to Twentymile Cascades on your right at mile 0.7. Climb moderately, passing over Twentymile Creek on wide bridges at mile 1.4 and 1.6. Just beyond the second crossing is the Twentymile Creek backcountry campsite, #93. Cross another bridge at the back of the campsite. The trail climbs above the creek, then drops down and crosses Twentymile Creek twice more on bridges, before coming to Proctor Gap at mile 3.0.

Stay forward on the old railroad bed and pick up the Long Hungry Ridge Trail, crossing Proctor Creek at mile 3.1. Swing around the point of a ridge, then come alongside Twentymile Creek again. The rotting bridges on the side streams are remnants of the railroad-logging era. These bridges are dangerous! Do not attempt to cross the creek using them. At mile 4.1, come to the Upper Flats backcountry campsite, #92 (elevation 2,520 feet). This is your first night's destination. Upper Flats has several good tent sites from which to choose. Large rocks emerge from the ground, forming natural seats at the campsite.

Start day two by immediately crossing Twentymile Creek, then Rye Patch Branch. The once moderate grade becomes steep as the trail crosses Rye Patch Branch at mile 4.6 of your loop hike. It then ascends the dry ridgeside. After a sharp right turn, come to Rye Patch (elevation 4,500 feet) at mile 6.8. This once open area is rapidly growing over but still remains an ideal resting spot after you've made the climb to the crest of Long Hungry Ridge.

Once atop the ridge, the last 0.8 mile of the Long Hungry Ridge Trail is easy, ending at the Gregory Bald Trail junction at mile 7.6. Turn left on the Gregory Bald Trail and shortly come to Rich Gap and another trail junction at mile 7.7. If you are thirsty, take the un-marked side trail to the left that swings 0.3 mile to Moore Spring, the site of an old Appalachian Trail shelter. Re-turning to Rich Gap, continue forward on the Gregory Bald Trail and climb 0.6 mile to the grassy meadow of Gregory Bald at mile 8.3. The bald, maintained at its present 15-acre size by the park service, offers a nearly

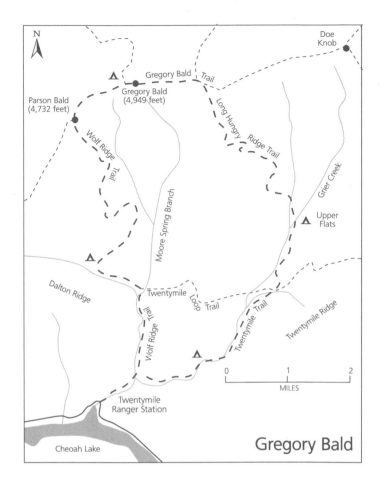

N

Doe
Knob

Gregory Bald
Trail

Gregory Bald
(4,949 feet)

Parson Bald
(4,732 feet)

Wolf Ridge
Trail

Long Hungry Ridge Trail

Grier Creek

Moore Spring Branch

Upper
Flats

Dalton Ridge

Twentymile
Loop Trail

Twentymile Trail

Twentymile Ridge

Wolf Ridge Trail

0   1   2

MILES

Twentymile
Ranger Station

Cheoah Lake

Gregory Bald

360-degree view. Flame azaleas bloom in June and blueberries follow after that.

Reenter the woods on the western end of the bald,
and descend to the Wolf Ridge Trail junction and the
Sheep Pen Gap backcountry campsite, #13 (elevation
4,560 feet), at mile 8.7. This is your second night's destination, a grassy glade of open level woodland, one of
the Smokies' finest backcountry campsites. Water can
be obtained by walking 200 yards down the Gregory
Bald Trail to a spring on your left. Sunset from atop
Gregory Bald is a Smoky Mountain sight not to be
missed.

Start day three by heading southwest on the Wolf
Ridge Trail through level woodland with a grassy
ground cover. Come to Parson Bald at mile 9.5 of your

loop hike. This bald, unlike Gregory Bald, is not maintained by the park service and is growing in rapidly with trees and bushes, which limit views. But over your left shoulder as you enter the bald stands the grassy field of Gregory Bald. Leave the bald and continue a nearly level hike for another 0.8 mile, then begin an irregular but steep descent down Wolf Ridge.

Swing right toward Dalton Branch, coming to the side trail leading to the Dalton Branch backcountry campsite, #95, at mile 13.1. Veer left beyond the campsite and pick up an old road that descends steeply to the Twentymile Loop Trail junction at mile 14.1. Ford Moore Spring Branch at mile 14.2 and 14.4. In the next 0.7 mile cross Moore Spring Branch three times on footlogs, to arrive at the Twentymile Trail junction at mile 15.1. Cross Moore Spring Branch a final time just beyond the junction and follow the Twentymile Trail 0.6 mile to the trailhead, completing your loop.

Directions: From Townsend, Tennessee, take US 321 north to the Foothills Parkway. Follow Foothills Parkway west to US 129. Follow US 129 south into North Carolina. Turn left on NC 28. Follow NC 28 for 2.6 miles to the Twentymile Ranger Station, on your left. Park beyond the ranger station and walk up to the gated road and begin your hike on the Twentymile Trail. From the courthouse in Bryson City, North Carolina, take US 19 south for 5.4 miles to NC 28. Follow NC 28 for 30 miles to reach the Twentymile Ranger Station, which will be on your right.

Smoky Mountain Reading List

Great Smoky Mountains, by Rose Houk. Boston: Houghton Mifflin Company, 1993.

This up-to-date natural history guide to the park reads like a storybook yet imparts fascinating scientific facts that tie together the complex web of life and land. Houk delves into the geology, flora and fauna, detailing the unique features that make the Smokies so special.

Hikers Guide to the Smokies, by Dick Murless and Constance Stallings. San Francisco: Sierra Club Books, 1973.

This is a Smokies classic. Though some of the information is outdated, the guidebook details Smokies trails and advises readers how to tramp through the mountains most wisely. A highly recommended book that is out of print and can be difficult to find.

Hiking Trails of the Smokies, edited by Steve Kemp. Gatlinburg, Tennessee: Great Smoky Mountains Natural History Association, 1993.

Offering a detailed description of every marked and maintained trail in the park, this is the latest comprehensive guide available. Written by more than a dozen trail enthusiasts, it includes an elevation profile graph for every trail and interesting information about the areas that the trails pass through.

Our Southern Highlanders, by Horace Kephart. Knoxville, Tennessee: University of Tennessee Press, 1984.

Originally published in 1913, this book describes the life of pioneers in and around the Smokies. Painfully honest, Kephart separates myth from reality on such subjects as bear hunting, moonshining and feuds. This book offers a real taste of life in the nineteenth century.

Smoky Mountains Hiking & Camping, by Lee Barnes. Birmingham, Alabama: Menasha Ridge Press, 1994.

This book is an excellent primer on the park. Barnes offers suggestions for what to do in every section of the park, while detailing certain trails and roads and bicycling and picnicking areas. This book helps you function both in and out of the park, giving important information concerning park regulations, accommodations and more.

Smoky Mountains Trout Fishing Guide, by Don Kirk. Birmingham, Alabama: Menasha Ridge Press, 1993.

Any angler who plies the 500 fishable miles of streams in the Smokies should consider this book as essential as a rod and reel. In a well-organized and informative fashion, Kirk offers tips to help anglers take on the fish that inhabit the mountain streams and lakes of the Smoky Mountains.

Strangers in High Places, by Michael Frome. Knoxville, Tennessee: University of Tennessee Press, 1980.

This book is the story of the Smoky Mountains as they have been shaped by those who entered them, from the Cherokees to the pioneers, from the loggers to the proponents of the idea of a national park. The most notable figures are closely detailed. Any Smokies enthusiast should have this book on the shelf.

Trees of the Smokies, edited by Steve Kemp. Gatlinburg, Tennessee: Great Smoky Mountains Natural History Association, 1993.

This guidebook describes the true stars of the Smokies, the trees. Excellent color photographs accompany each description of where to find and how to identify the species that inhabit the park. Compact in size, this book is a joy on the trail.

Trial by Trail: Backpacking in the Smokies, by Johnny Molloy. Knoxville, Tennessee: University of Tennessee Press, 1996.

Follow hiker Molloy as he explores the park through

true backpacking adventures. He weaves Smokies facts and lore along with practical backpacking tips and glimpses of his growth as a woodsman. This book offers his experiences of the highs and lows of life on the trail.

A Wonderment of Mountains: The Great Smokies, by Carson Brewer. Knoxville, Tennessee: Tenpenny Publishing, 1981.

Smokies authority Brewer has compiled a selection of his best columns of the mountains he loves. History, hiking, pioneers and other aspects of the Smokies are covered in this book that can be read time and again.

Index